Critical acclaim for Sunetra Gupta

'This outstanding novel is both an elegy for Bengali culture and for the genre of romance itself; a poetic study of decay and dislocation, it is also woven around fables that can never be destroyed because they are never wholly real' *Spectator*

'Haunting and poignant, *A Sin of Colour* is a brilliant piece of writing in which the author weaves a vivid tapestry from the multi-coloured strands which mirror the lives of her characters as they move between Calcutta, London, Oxford and New York. Her luminous prose evokes a deeply moving picture of a family torn apart by bitterness, jealousy and unrequited passion' *Historical Novels Review*

'A prodigious talent' *Independent on Sunday*

'This is a beautifully written, luminous novel, filled with meticulous images that range across three continents and as many generations' *Glasgow Herald*

'A young, true heir to Virginia Woolf' *Kirkus Reviews*

'This novel vibrates with the tension of restrained passion . . . She manages to convey the emotions of the characters, subtly shifting from one viewpoint to another . . . She skilfully weaves the elements of the epic family story together, leaving us with an outcome at once unavoidable and yet unforeseen. *A Sin of Colour* is a wonderful kaleidoscope of mystery tension and passion' *Oxford Times*

Sunetra Gupta was born in Calcutta in 1965. She now lives in Oxford with her husband and two daughters and divides her time between writing and researching infectious diseases.

BY THE SAME AUTHOR

Memories of Rain
The Glassblower's Breath
Moonlight into Marzipan

A Sin of Colour

SUNETRA GUPTA

PHŒNIX

A PHOENIX PAPERBACK

First published in Great Britain by Phoenix House in 1999
This paperback edition published in 2000 by Phoenix,
an imprint of Orion Books Ltd,
Orion House, 5 Upper St Martin's Lane,
London WC2H 9EA

The title *A Sin of Colour* is taken from *A Hard Heart* by
Howard Barker with the kind permission of the playwright

Copyright © Sunetra Gupta 1999

The right of Sunetra Gupta to be identified as the author of
this work has been asserted by her in accordance with the
Copyright, Designs and Patents Act 1988.

A CIP catalogue record for this book
is available from the British Library.

ISBN: 0 75381 055 7

Printed and bound in Great Britain by
The Guernsey Press Co. Ltd, Guernsey, C.I.

To Isolde

AMETHYST

It was not far from the railway station to the boarding house and he was able to drag his trunk across the road and down the narrow street by halting every few steps to blow upon his frozen fingers, and allow himself to be briefly immersed in the perverse fantasy that he might never see her again. Perhaps his family would fall upon hard times and he would never be able to afford his passage home, spend the rest of his life slaving as a schoolmaster in some obscure corner of Britain, while she, his brother's wife, started giving private tuition in Music and English to make ends meet. Their grand home in Calcutta would have to be auctioned, and the heavy furniture crammed like a herd of tired elephants into a small flat. His father might have to share a room with his grandchildren, give up his expensive habits, resign from his clubs, spend lonely hours on a narrow balcony staring out onto the street while the children did their homework and their mother perspired over a small kerosene stove as she prepared their evening meal.

He remembered, as he often did, the angle of her elbow as she stirred some bubbling potion in the small kitchen she had set up in an alcove of her private drawing room, previously occupied by a creaky upright piano. It was in this room that he and his sisters had received their music lessons when they were children. But although she was a gifted musician, his brother's wife had never learnt the piano. She had had it removed and a hotplate and shelves installed in its place, and these she tended with such care that sometimes when he wandered in and his glance fell upon the rows of gleaming jars, the jaunty blue stove resting upon the slab of dark marble, he would feel that it had, in the stillness of the afternoon, the atmosphere of a

3

shrine. The piano lay gathering dust in the hallway. Sometimes he would play for her upon it the few Western classical pieces he knew, she had a virulent distaste for Indian music played on the piano, and even for the use of the instrument harmlessly to accompany Bengali songs. As he played, he would sense her every fragile movement among the great shadows, and yet another small part of him would be obliterated by a yearning to trace very gently with his fingers the outlines of her face, to lift from her cheek, upon a gnarled nail, one of her precious tears.

And here he was now, in distant Oxford, as far away from her as he ever might be, as ignorant of the true nature of her feelings for him as he was on the first day that he came to love her, for no words had ever passed between them nor ever would besides those they had speckled so purposefully with the affectionate banter deemed proper between a man and his elder brother's wife, as painful to him as an army of ragged claws upon his tongue.

A young woman answered the doorbell, coloured under his intense gaze, and called for her aunt. He was shown to his rooms, small and badly lit, with a faint but abiding smell of cold overboiled cabbage, and letting the trunk handles slip from his aching fingers he closed the door and seated himself upon the bed with his back to the whorled wallpaper, to drink of the chamber's still amber, and think of her, his brother's wife, Reba.

Before long there was a knock on the door. It was the same young woman, the landlady's niece, come to ask if he would like any refreshment, although it was long past the hour that they served breakfast. And so he found himself seated at the dining table before a pile of pale sandwiches, the September sun shining vehemently upon the frilly net curtains, and the landlady and her niece at the other end of the table sipping tea. He ate slowly, fingering the scalloped edges of the plate and wondering whether Reba would have approved of this piece of china or dismissed it as a cheap imitation, while the landlady

4

spoke of how chilly it was indeed for this time of the year, and her niece agreed with a shy turn of her cheek which felt, quite inexplicably, like an apple gently settling into his palm.

From that moment, Debendranath Roy began to nurture an uncertain inclination to touch the cheek that had turned so softly in hapless assent to his landlady's pronouncement about the weather, and although it never grew fully into a desire to possess and revere the person, the mild flutterings of his flesh on many an evening spent in her company provided a pleasantly ironical contrast to the dense dark meshes of the desire that he had enshrined in the dead cabbage smell of his own chamber, and to which he would return so gratefully every evening.

He had a photograph of his brother's family upon his desk, taken shortly after the birth of their daughter. In the photograph Reba held Niharika wrapped tightly in a shawl, while her twin sons stood on either side of her, and her husband behind her, gripping the back of her chair. Her face was turned to the infant, so that she appeared only in indistinct profile, and yet this was the one he had chosen of the two that he had been offered, he had chosen this one remarking that he particularly liked it for the impish expressions on his nephews' faces, and he had watched with cruel delight as her fingers had for a moment frozen upon the other photograph, where her face was very much more visible, which was the one she had thought he would be sure to choose.

Who are they? the landlady's niece had asked one evening as he helped her with her correspondence course in librarianship. Who are these beautiful children?

My nephews, he had replied.

Is the baby a boy as well? she had asked.

It is a little girl, he had told her.

She will be two years old tomorrow, he had added, for it was the twenty-third of November, and more than two months had passed since he had arrived in Oxford.

His landlady's niece reached out for the photograph. He

buried his gaze in a pile of her homework papers while she scrutinized it, trembling with mild anticipation, as if this incident might mark some vivid change in his existence, and when he raised his head again he found that she was dusting it with the corner of her handkerchief.

Jennifer, please – he said to her – please do not fiddle with my things.

I am sorry, she said, it was very dusty.

I like a bit of dust, he replied, relenting when she meant so well. But taking the frame from her hands, he saw that that she had simply rubbed the dust into the corners, the effect was to him somehow obscene. And in that moment he realized that he would rather that his whole life were left exactly as it was in that moment of terrible beauty when he had realized that he loved her as he would never love any other woman, for since then he had taken comfort in any form of desuetude, the heavy breath of old unpolished teak, the freckled edges of the old mirrors, the limechoked cisterns and the chipped ceramic, decay had become nectar to Debendranath Roy on the day that he discovered that he loved his brother's wife. Often he would watch the failing light disperse upon the fine sheen of dust that gathered upon her musical instruments by the evening, and wished that they themselves might be enwreathed forever in such a moist light. In the morning she would clean their gentle flanks herself, and practise upon her delicate *esraj* for many hours, her dark eyes focussed upon a point so distant that when he had first watched her perform, as a young college student, it had given meaning to the peculiar notion that infinity was where two parallel lines meet. There was not a day when she did not practise her *esraj* in the early hours, waking before dawn if her other duties were likely to consume most of the morning, it was only at the time of his mother's death that for weeks she did not touch her musical instruments, felt it inappropriate even to cover them, and he had seen her cast her eyes upon them with a longing that stirred within him a keen envy towards the inanimate objects, and then in her absence he had approached them, blown the dust off their smooth and complex surfaces, and sheathed them carefully in their cotton jackets, and sat beside their slumbering forms as a man might sit, at her funeral, with the children of a woman he once loved.

And who is she? asked Jennifer, of the one other photograph he kept in open view upon his desk.

My mother, he replied.

She looks sad, observed Jennifer.

She was sad, he confirmed, although I never knew it, not until just before she died.

And how did you know it then? she asked.

And he told her of his mother's madness, how it had started with small things, faint emulations of her daughter-in-law's habits, how his mother who had always been grandly indifferent to all household affairs had started ordering new covers for her drawing room chairs, and making trips to the Jewish bakery to buy cakes for their afternoon tea, she who had never taken the slightest interest in their diet when they were children. At first they tried to ignore the change within her, as flowers appeared in vases in her bedroom, pictures on the walls. Quite unexpectedly they realized that she, so refined in spirit, had hardly any taste at all when it came to material things. Never before, after all, had she been called upon to display any sophistication in such matters – she had gone through life without the burden of decorating her own home, or even selecting her own wardrobe, most of her clothes were gifts, or had been chosen by her mother-in-law many years ago. And here she was, without warning, seeking to master those precious talents by which Reba had put her stamp upon the set of rooms that had been allotted to her and her husband. Like Reba, she ordered paintings on silk, and jewellery boxes of Kashmiri craftwork, and he could only watch in horror as the bare dignity of his parents' chambers died a swift death under the motley onslaught of such doubtful treasures. And then came the day when he returned in the evening to find her busily instructing the carpenter to put shelves outside her drawing room where the long corridor turned and came to an end, so that she too might have a small kitchen of her own, I need jars and some pans, she said, looking up at him from the floor where she sat fiddling with a small kerosene stove, and it was then that he realized that his mother had gone mad.

It was a swift madness, and ended soon with her quietly dying in bed beside his father. Like a moth that had hit the ceiling fan and fallen upon the pillow, never to move again, she lay, serene once more, pale and cold again was her unanguished brow, and he could only be grateful that her death had been as delicate as much of her life, and that the frenzy of the past few months might be forgotten, and never come to dull the fragrance of her memory. Meanwhile they dressed her in redbordered white, smeared quantities of vermilion into the parting of her hair, and sent her almost as a bride to her pyre, their beautiful mother, his silent ally of so many years.

And at first he had hated her, his brother's wife Reba, for coming into their lives and distorting it in such an unpredictable manner, for driving his mother towards such an undignified end, to die with the taste of her burnt efforts at mango chutney upon her tongue, she who should have passed by degrees into delicious oblivion, on the firm and faded course that had been selected as her fate from the moment that his father, Indranath Roy, had first set eyes upon her, walking back from school in a small North Bengal town, regal in unbleached homespun, a thick black braid falling across the pale arch of her shoulder. Who is she? his father had asked the mill manager. The young girl with the books, who is she?

She was the daughter of the local doctor, his father had learnt presently, from a family of strong ideals, moderate means and many daughters. She was the most beautiful of them, and it was rumoured that she was doing extremely well at school. Her mother had plans to send to send her to college in Dhaka, and though her father was reluctant that she should leave home unless to become a suitable man's wife, he had never been known to contradict his wife on any matter, so the

8

neighbours said, and it seemed only fair that such a bright young girl should go to college, it was not as if it was unheard of these days, so the neighbours had judged between mouthfuls of betelnut, fanning away flies in that unusually warm November of 1931.

From North Bengal, Indranath Roy had journeyed into the foothills of the Himalayas, to seek out the Japanese Cedars, with which they would line their new make of wardrobes – one of these they later had in their bedroom, and whenever she opened it, the room would fill with the fragrance of his shapeless desire to know and possess her.

At the end of the week, while drinking tea with the mill manager in his hotel room, Indranath Roy had asked him if he knew her name.

You are still thinking of her? the mill manager had asked in disbelief.

Some things are meant to be, he had replied.

Four months later he returned to her home town with a dusty entourage piping 'It's a long long way to Tipperary', to marry her. The groom and his party were borne on palanquins from the railway station, past the dry paddy fields, the curious eyes of peasant children huddling in patches of winter sun, a madwoman spitting guava seeds, to the village doctor's humble home, where his bride sat waiting, famished and decorated, her younger sisters busily gobbling sweets and playing hopscotch in the vast marquee, and her elder sister by her side staring wistfully at her painted feet. Your turn will come, she assured her, your turn will come.

Mother will miss you so dreadfully, said her sister, it will be miserable when you are gone.

I wish they could have waited, she said bitterly, at least till after my exams. It had been arranged that she would appear as a private candidate for her school leaving exams in Calcutta. She had her admission card tucked away in her trunk, had almost fainted with relief when it had arrived in the post the week before. She had been assigned a seat at a famous convent school, not very far, her father assured her, from what would be her new home, the grand villa that her future husband had recently purchased from a departing Englishman, and rechristened 'Mandalay' for he had made a vast fortune in Burma teak. Later, as she watched the unslept night pass like broken china between her fingers, her new husband, pacing by the window, would attempt to convince her that she need not be ashamed of his wealth.

What I have gained from this world is not incommensurate with what I have given it, he told her. We have always taken good care of our peasants, and now we take good care of our workers, our craftsmen. We are building a new school for the peasants' children, if you like you can go and visit it when we are in the country. We could even start a girls' school, and name it, he said tenderly, after you.

She sat with lowered eyes, his words drifting like clots of milk through the murk of her mind. Would you like that? he persisted, to have a school named after you – The Srimati Neerupama Roy Girls' Primary School – would that please you? he asked.

The sudden shock of her new name caused her to tremble under her heavy garments, but she nodded her jewelled head twice to indicate that yes, indeed, it would please her, to have a girls' school named after her.

He laughed a low triumphant laugh. I will make you very happy, he told her. And though she never gave him this pleasure, not once in the thirty-five years that they lived as man and wife did he ever feel he had made her happy, he never ceased to be grateful to her for appearing to him on that distant day in the winter of 1931, her schoolbooks clutched against her bosom, her lovely eyes dipped against the low rays of afternoon sun, it was an image that he would feast upon until the day of his death, many years after she had left this world, and longer still since she had withdrawn from it into unfathomable depths of her own. Between him and her private kingdom was a wall of terrifying silence, and yet more ravishing than ever was she, he sometimes thought, in her splendid seclusion, in her voluptuous indifference to her role as mistress of his splendid home, as the mother of his five children, as his beloved wife.

Sometimes, it frightened him a little that although she loved her children, nowhere in her affections was a hint of the manic tenderness that he had always associated with motherhood. She read them endless fairytales, guided their homework, watched over them when they were ill, but her concern for them never seemed to stray beyond the rational, she would calmly swab the pus from a ghastly wound and dress it as her father had taught her many years ago, and when the child winced she would lay a firm hand upon its head, and kiss its brow, but not once did he see tears in her own eyes for the small sufferings of the flesh of her own flesh. It was as if she had decided to accept motherhood without any of its agony, and had somehow succeeded.

Within a year of their marriage they had been blessed with a son, cast very much in his father's image, only lighter, like his mother, in complexion, and softer somewhat of jaw. With him, at least, she had been dutifully engrossed, especially as there had been no other children for a good five years, after which were born in quick succession three daughters and another son. For this last birth, she could not return to her parents' home as she had done for the rest of them, for they were deep into the War by then, and the railroads were no longer safe. Indranath Roy had despatched her, with the children, to their country estate in the east, a land of rivers, and perpetual flood. It was there that, on a night of heavy rain, Debendranath Roy made his way bravely into the world, while she fell immediately into a terrible fever, her blood corrupted by his strenuous birth. Eventually, she recovered, but was faded and frail for many months even after they returned to Calcutta. So angelic was she in her illness that Indranath Roy felt it would be obscene to lay his hands upon her, except perhaps simply to soothe her brow, and gradually it became more and more remote a possibility that he should inflict upon her his cruel male needs, pierce through the layers of mute suffering with his acid lust, until soon it seemed almost inconceivable that his devotion to her might ever have been ennobled by desire.

Still, some part of him suspected that he had stifled something within her, and in 1951, he made a last vain attempt to rekindle her spirits by taking her on a trip to Europe. It was a promise he had made to her in the first tender year of their marriage, a promise that he was still eager to keep, and even she, for the first time in many years, seemed somewhat enthused by the prospect of travelling to the lands that she had dreamt of so often as a child, that had come alive to her in the books that she had devoured then, come alive with the insistence of a lost past, locking her into histories that were not hers, that ran alive still like a quick river beneath mute rocks, and dipping her hand down through them after all these years she was startled at its force. She packed her warm shawls and long-sleeved blouses into a trunk, and asked her sister-in-law to accompany her to Lindsay Street in search of an appropriate overcoat.

But the long journey by ship took the steam out of her emotions, the endless expanse of ocean stretched her thoughts again to a gossamer web, where all that had once mattered clung like fine dust. By the time they arrived in London, she was already weary, and longing to be back within the cool walls of their home in Calcutta, where since the death of her mother-in-law just after the War, she had lived in solid imperturbable calmness. Before her marriage, she had seen her life sweated out in the blood and thunder of crisis, she had felt she must devote herself to delivering her people from the yoke of poverty, from colonial oppression, the injustices of feudalism, she had seen herself as a village schoolteacher, teaching women to read and write in the evening by the light of kerosene lamps, insects buzzing thickly around, she had seen herself waking before dawn to walk to the railway station and catch the train to town in time for a political rally, she had thought she might fall in love with some dedicated revolutionary, who might appear suddenly at her home in between two critical missions, and she would feed him whatever she had in the house, sit by his side and fan him while he ate what could be his last meal, and then he would briefly and tenderly touch her cheek and vanish into the night, that is how she had thought it might be. And instead she had become the wife of a timber merchant, mother to five well-fed children, and so little besides. And yet it was not as if there were no avenues open to her as a rich man's wife to better the lot of the unfortunate millions. That had been one of the arguments her father had used to get her to agree to the marriage – think of how much you will be able to do for others with your wealth, he had said – think of what you might achieve, my sweet, just think of it. Certainly, her husband had been closely involved with whom he considered the more respectable of Nationalists, had donated extensively to their movement, but he had made no attempt to include her in any of it, and it had not been obvious to her where exactly she might have found a niche. That was all history now, with the War over, and Independence gained. Partition had forced her father to pack his belongings and move his large family to Calcutta, where they lived now upon the southern fringes of the city, struggling to make ends meet, too proud to accept any offers of money from her or her husband except the occasional college fee, a lavish birthday gift, the loan of a car to take someone to hospital, but nothing more. It intrigued Indranath Roy that his wife did not spend more time in charity work, like other ladies in her position. Now that her children were grown, how was it, he thought, that she, who had shown such interest in the early years of their marriage in the fate of their people, how was it that she, brimming with passion as she had been then for their suffering, was now so indifferent to the workings of the world without, that it should matter so little to her what passed beyond the high walls of their garden, that she should be content to sit and sew all afternoon under the shade of the fig trees, her children frolicking about her or fallen asleep on the grass, a heavenly tableau. Watching them from his office window he would often feel that he was looking through a telescope, that these were glimpses of an ethereal reality of which he was master, over which he exercised an intangible authority, but could only savour from a distance.

It had been a great relief to him when his son married, and young Reba came into the household, quiet and dignified, and yet so much more of a feminine presence, he felt, than his wife, who more and more had retreated into the shadowed corners of her self, each day a little paler, like a faded mosaic, only rushing temporarily into relief when washed by sudden water, but then drying again into subtle delectable outlines. Reba, he felt, was no less composed than her mother-in-law, but hummed with a temperate womanly energy, transforming her corner of the great house into a region of easy beauty, with flowerpots on the balcony, and framed Moghul miniatures on the walls. Her tiny kitchen was always kept so prettily, stocked with meticulous jars of spices and dried fruits, her gleaming vessels carefully piled with layers of muslin in between. She would effortlessly turn out the most delicious of savouries for their tea, bake cakes to take to orphanages and to the Old People's Home on Lower Circular Road. Here was a woman, he felt, who was engaged with the world, in her own small ways, as a woman should be, here was a woman who radiated grace, while his wife only dwelt within her own luminosity, drawing inwards the music that should have streamed forth from her, sucking into herself the harmony of her movements that had drawn him to her, that summer day, so many years ago, when he had watched her walking home from school through the dust, her head bent, her books clasped to her bosom, her black braid swinging gently upon her back.

Indeed, everyone was quite besotted with Reba, but Deben-dranath Roy, who flinched in loyal resentment from her alien presence which was consuming their household, who clung fiercely to the old order with his silent mother at its centre. And when she too began to crumble under the spirit of this strange woman, he locked himself in his room, and gave himself to intense study, shutting out what was happening within the great and silent halls of his childhood, outside his barred door. It was only after the twins were born, and emerged from behind the solid veil of servants that had screened their infancy, it was only then that Debendranath Roy was drawn back out of his cocoon, and began to spend his afternoons chasing lizards with his nephews, while Reba retreated with the fatigue of a second pregnancy following close upon the heels of the first. He had hardly seen or spoken to her in the three years she had been married to his brother, and although the excitement surrounding her had eroded to a degree with time, somewhere in this house his mother was still quietly going mad, all because of her. Soon the time would come for her to leave for her father's house for the remainder of her confinement, the small dusty flat, thick with books and sheaves of music, where he had first set eyes upon her, three years ago, when he had come to pass judgement on her suitability as a bride for his elder brother.

And so it happened that one morning he came down to play with his nephews and found them dressed to accompany their mother to her parents' home, where they would stay for a good six months or so. This was the tradition, and he had found it most annoying as a schoolboy that at least one of his three sisters was usually staying with them for this reason. He resented the scent of anxiety that hung around childbirth, the relentless flapping of women around the newborn, and the sullen swollen movements of his sisters that made him feel they were already bored with their roles as mothers and wives. He was apprehensive, when he first went to visit his nephews at Reba's parents' flat, that he might find her too in such a condition, for the new baby was only three weeks old. He had never visited her after the birth of the twins, although he had been curious to see if they were identical or not, and even this time, it was his nephews that he was here to see, not the mother or the infant. Indeed he wished not to see her at all if she was in that strange oozy state of new motherhood that he had seen in his sisters. Instead he found her seated on a rush mat on a square patch of winter sun with her father's *tanpura* singing a Tagore song about the devotion of a dancer to the Lord Buddha, whom she knows not how to worship except through dance,

> Forgive me this, but just to think of you makes me fill
>   with the nectar of dance
> With all my consciousness, and all my exquisite
>   anguish, I will make you an offering,
> Let it not die of shame at your feet,
> For I have neither fruit nor flower to offer you
>   otherwise,
> Nor any holy water in my vessel.

It is you, she said, with surprise, when she saw him. But the boys have just gone out, she said, guessing that he was here to see her sons.

I can come back another time, he said.

Surely you will stay and have some tea?

Only if you will continue your singing, he said. He had hardly ever spoken to her directly before. I have never heard you sing, he said.

I can only sing if I am alone, she said.

Then I will go.

As you wish, she said, smiling very slightly, her eyes upon a mangy cat staring pleadingly at her from a neighbouring rooftop. I have forgotten to save any scraps for her, she said slowly.

Are you well? he heard himself ask.

I am, she said, and you?

I am well, he said, but I miss the boys.

Just another month or two, she said, and then they will be returned to you.

And suddenly he realized how much she must dislike their home, how she must hate its sterile interior, the furniture that had no meaning, no history, no past, while in her father's home, even the threadbare tablecloth had its dignity, bookshelves towered graciously above them everywhere spilling well-thumbed books, and the moth-eaten armchairs were steeped in the memories of a departed age.

He thought of her, as she might have stood in her new maidenhood, at the tall window, and looked out upon the row of shanties that knelt against the walls of their neighbour's house. He thought of her as she might have been then, before she acquired her formidable composure, her endless accomplishments, the ability to diminish anyone with a slight slant of her eyes. He thought of her as she might have been, in her secluded and lonely girlhood as the only daughter of a renowned professor of Ancient Indian History and his ailing wife. He had been told that because her mother was bedbound, it was she who had accompanied her father to many of his engagements, that she had been able to discourse freely with his friends, many years her senior, at a remarkably young age, for the rest of the time reading voraciously. All this he had been told, and yet, in the three years that she had lived with them as his brother's wife, he had never heard her pass a single opinion on any matter, even though she had mesmerized everyone with her grace and dignity, with her artistic and musical talents. He had never heard her comment upon anything of consequence. He had been impressed that she had a First Class Bachelor's degree in Sanskrit, but beyond that, he had had no evidence of her learning. And looking at her now, he realized that there had been no occasion at all where they might have seen who she was beyond a beautiful woman who decorated her rooms nicely, baked excellent cakes, played exceptionally well on the *esraj*, and could scorn a person's indelicacy of manner with the faintest tilt of her eyebrows. At dinner the conversation was dominated by his father and elder brother, mostly about their business, and occasionally politics. In any case, she hardly ever spoke in the presence of her father-in-law, kept her head covered and her eyes lowered as befitted a young bride. And although she practised religiously upon her musical instruments every morning, this was the first time he had heard her sing anything other than a lullaby. I do not know her, he decided, I do not know her at all.

He saw her as she sat upon the rush mat, her thick hair fanned out over her back, her fingers running soundlessly along the strings of her father's *tanpura*, and realized suddenly how lonely she must feel within the walls of his home, how sad the prospect of returning to her husband's home where she was so respected and valued, so adored. He saw her staring out through the window at the steel noon sky, and felt there was nothing so beautiful as her loneliness.

He felt that she had filled her life with many things and yet not filled it at all, that within her was a vast empty space, sacred and untouchable, for she had found nothing yet that was worthy of inhabiting it, despite all her knowledge and her wisdom, and all her rich and tender links to the dead and the living, she had found nothing to adorn these recesses, and in scenting their starkness he felt as if he were gazing upon the cavernous ruins of a great city, where he might lose himself without any regret.

He had not come to see her, and yet, within these few moments, her presence had acquired a meaning that he had never imagined it might come to have, and before he knew it she had risen and taken her leave of him, before he had had the chance to say anything more. Her father came out onto the veranda and seated himself upon the wicker recliner across from him. The maid had brought them tea, and he managed to answer her father's questions about his studies intelligently, but all the while his mind was overrun by the sound of her humming somewhere inside the network of bedrooms the song that he had interrupted, *my supplication is in my song and in my gestures of dance, forgive me this, and bless me nonethe-less, for every thought of you fills me with the nectar of dance,* while the world roared around him, he heard little but the faint strains of this melody, in whose depths he had first come face to face with the sublime expanse of her loneliness.

It was this that he still celebrated, in the welcome dark of his two damp rooms in his boarding house in Oxford, the luminosity of her loneliness. For although he had trespassed upon these solemn territories, he had feared but to tread very lightly upon the hinterland between her inner and outer selves, and for him, that had been enough. He knew that if he ever had the opportunity to shelter her, it was not all of her that he would seek to know, but only those few inlets where her loneliness pushed through and attempted to meet the world, and that would be enough.

He wanted to imagine a number of things, mostly impossible fantasies. More than any of these he simply wanted to imagine what it might be like to touch her hands, to stroke her long fingers, one by one, she wore no rings for she claimed they interfered with her playing, her nails were always slightly stained with turmeric, and she would never think of varnishing them as he had seen his sisters do, hours spent giggling and screaming with dabs of cottonwool, and the strange acrid smell of nail polish remover in their bedroom. How different Reba's childhood must have been among those noiseless bookladen walls, alone, with her mother sleeping in her sick-room, and her father deep in his papers, and the maids whispering softly in the kitchen as they cleared up after lunch. It must have been in such a time that she had invented herself. From elements of the novels she had devoured in her childish loneliness, from images obliquely prescribed to her by her father and his friends, from the colours and odours of the silences around her, she had made herself. He saw it as a sequence of deliberate decisions, but oddly found no dishonesty in this, even though he himself had just become who he was without much thought to the process. He had grown effortlessly into manhood only to dissolve piece by piece under her gaze.

And here he was now, far far away, tutoring himself to cherish without agony what little he had of her, she who could never be his, and from whom he had never had any indication that she might want to exchange her life for one with him at its centre. Except perhaps on that windy day when they had taken the twins to a country fair in Shantiniketan, and wandering there among the colourful stalls with the boys, riding together on the Ferris wheel, and buying them candyfloss, they had been bound in an almost matrimonial harmony. She had purchased a necklace at a tribal stall and held it out silently for him to fasten about her neck, as if this, and much else, was already understood between them, and yet, by the time they returned to the guest house, the distance between them had returned, the spell was broken, she was once again his brother's wife.

It had not been an unbroken adoration, there were women at college, and later at university whom he was occasionally drawn to, at times he had almost been convinced that these were more real than his obsession with her, but then he would wake at dawn to sounds of her practising on her *esraj*, and something in the desperation of its tone would make him feel that she knew he had betrayed her, and later when he encountered the young woman who had momentarily distracted him, he would meet her covertly fond looks with impenetrable ice. With Jennifer, however, this did not have the desired effect, so habituated was she to unkindness. Even if he ignored her at breakfast, she would still look for a smile in the evening when she brought him his glass of cheap port in the living room. The first time that he had shown any chilliness to her in the morning, he had regretted it all day, for he had realized how dear to him was her humble devotion. It depressed him to think that she might never show any tenderness towards him again, for the women he had known in Calcutta had all been too proud to persevere against even the slightest discouragement. On the way back to the boarding house, he had bought her a small bunch of daffodils. He found her in the dining room, working at her correspondence course, she took off her glasses as soon as she saw him, for she thought they made her look ugly, these are for you, he told her, leaving the flowers upon the table instead of putting them in her hands, these are for you, he said, and then turned around and walked out of the room, mounted the stairs to his own rooms, and locked the door. Some years later he would find the flowers pressed to dry paper between the leaves of an encyclopaedia. He had found the dessicated flowers while unpacking their boxes in their new home in Highgate, where he had found a teaching job. It had been their intention after they were married to live in Calcutta, but this had somehow not been possible, for reasons that she would never know. They had only lived in Mandalay a year when he decided that they should return to England, and so, with tears in her eyes she had packed their bags, reswathed their wedding presents in newspaper, and left with him the following morning, hardly as the sun had risen, left without saying goodbye to anyone, not even the children whom she had come to love. She had glanced for the last time in the direction of their rooms, but all she could hear were the sounds of their mother practising upon her musical instrument. He was about to follow her into the taxi, but then he stopped, walked back into the house as if he had forgotten something. And then he returned, his eyes rimmed with a heavenly grief that he sought to hide from her throughout the journey by pretending much of the time to be asleep. For it was to Reba that he had gone to say farewell, he had come and stood at her door, her back was to him as she played, but she sensed his presence in the half dark, and lowered the *esraj* onto her lap, have you come to say goodbye, she asked, turning her head so that he could see her in profile, have you come to say goodbye?

I have, he replied.

Why must you creep away? she asked. Why must you steal away like a sorry thief when you could go otherwise?

Why is it you so abhor any kind of weakness in a man? he asked her. If this is how I feel I should go, why do you wish to deny me a coward's exit?

Because you will regret it, she replied.

I will not regret it.

You disappoint me, she said, staring straight ahead, away from him.

That is all I ever seem to do, he said, very softly to the back of her head, and then when she turned around again, he was there no longer. She heard the engine of the taxi start outside, and then he was gone.

The year before he had written to her: *You will be pleased to know that I am marrying an English girl. I am relying upon you to break this news to my father. You have always managed these things better than the rest of us.* She had lifted her dark eyes from the page, and watched her husband struggling with his braces. Your brother is marrying a memsaheb, she had told him, in a voice like cold tea, good for him, her husband had replied, she watched him amble out into the dark dining hall, grab a slice of cake from the pile that lay under the cooling fan for her to take that afternoon to the Old People's Home on Lower Circular Road, she looked for a long while at her own reflection in the closet mirror, studied the arch of her eyebrows, one slightly higher than the other, gazed upon the comforting economy of her lower lip, the long thin bow of the upper, she folded the letter into a tight bruised square, and tucked it under the mattress, she heard voices in the garden, her children had come home from school.

I am marrying an English girl, he had written, seated at his desk, shaking his weary fountain pen for drops of life, until Jennifer had appeared, an unsummoned ghost with a bottle of royal blue and some toilet tissue to catch the excesses of inkthirst, only to be waved away – I never use blue ink, he had told her, you should know that by now. And she had retreated, as she always would, in the face of his sudden cruelties, knowing that if she waited quietly downstairs, he would eventually appear, strangely penitent, as if guilty of some much larger crime than just having snapped at her a few minutes ago. There was something so warm and gentle about his grief that she was glad to be enveloped by it, even though she suspected that only a very small part of it was connected with her at all.

That Indian man seems to be particularly fond of you, her aunt had observed while she helped her cook breakfast.

He wants to marry me, she muttered, laying strips of bacon on the skillet.

I can't imagine why, her aunt replied.

Nor can I, she said.

Well, that's you sorted then, said her aunt.

You will have to find someone else to help you, she said.

That's easily done.

I'm sorry to spring this on you so suddenly, she said.

Where will you get married?

Just in Oxford, I think, she said, just at the registrar's, you know.

We can have the reception here, said her aunt.

Oh no, she said, we wouldn't want to trouble you.

No trouble, said her aunt, it's not as if you get married every day.

Oh, Auntie Mabel, she said, you are so kind to me.

You are burning the bacon, said her aunt.

On the eve of the wedding, after Debendranath Roy had gone to bed, she and her aunt sat in the kitchen and decorated the cake. While she piped roses onto the uneven icing, her aunt produced from a paper bag a small plastic tiger to place next to the figures of the bride and groom, seeing as he is from Bengal, she said. Jennifer held the small figure of the bride in her fingers and sighed that she was not to be in splendid white on the morrow, nor he in top hat and tails like the little groom, which is how she had always imagined it after all. Nothing mattered really except to be forever with him, she had consoled herself, to live quietly by his side forever, waiting in the evenings patiently for him to return from the library, and on the days when he stayed in, to raise her eyes from her sewing to his tall back stooped over his desk, to bring him the endless cups of tea that he liked to drink, and sit with him upon the arm of his chair as he watched cricket, sometimes even trying to explain to her the peculiar rules of the game. What more could she possibly want, she asked herself. And so the following afternoon they assembled with a handful of relatives and friends at the Town Hall, and someone handed her a bouquet of tigerlilies that he glanced at in mild distaste, or so she imagined, as they were called in to take their vows, to sign their dissonant names upon the dotted lines. And then they had trooped back to this house to eat sandwiches and porkpies and scotch eggs and cake and drink a glass of sparkling wine. But then he had refused to cut the cake with her, even though her friends had pleaded and pleaded, and she had stood redfaced by the door, ready to dash to the bathroom, should the tears that she had kept so far in check come to stream inconsiderately from her eyes, as they often did, in the worst of situations, though no situation could be much worse than this, she had thought, as he glared across at her from within a circle of her friends, all trying desperately to convince him to have a picture taken of them cutting the cake together. It's the sort of thing you'll want later to show your children, she heard one of them say.

She turned away, gulping back her tears, and heard a man's voice admonishing her friends. Leave him alone for God's sake, leave him alone. The voice belonged to Tom, from her home town, working now as a builder in Oxford. It was Tom they had thought she would marry at first, for he had courted her after a fashion, especially just after she had arrived in Oxford, taking her to the movies, or just for a walk on Port Meadow. He had once even taken her to Blenheim palace. But some part of her had always been stifled by Tom, and memories of home, and perhaps he sensed this, for his visits grew more infrequent, although sometimes he would turn up unexpectedly in a new set of clothes or a new car, and beg her aunt's permission to whisk her off to a party or for a drive in the Cotswolds. Watching her from his window once, being helped into a bright sports car by this muscular youth, Debendranath Roy had felt a strange hotness which he was forced to identify as jealousy. That he should be jealous now seemed absurd to him, when for so many years he had endured someone else's possession of the only woman he could ever love. Could it be, he wondered, some hideous remnant of a patrilocal consciousness that Reba was already part of his family, and belonged in some sense, collectively, to them? But no, it would not have mattered if she were the wife of a friend, or even an enemy, the truth was that she could never be any man's property, neither his burden nor his reward.

There had been times when he had sought for himself something other than a lifetime of the agony of loving her, and never more so than when in his third and last year in Oxford he had found himself smitten by an Israeli graduate student by the name of Amira. She was exceptionally beautiful, and for some weeks he found himself wandering the stone corridors and the cobbled streets with her name always whispering in his ear, Amira, Amira, Amira, and then wondrously she invited him to dinner at the house she shared on Iffley Road with two other students, fed him a marvellous broth, and with much wine and good conversation, and the evening ending by him singing Tagore songs by candlelight to all three of them, Debendranath Roy had briefly thought that this might be the true shape of the life that lay ahead. He had returned to the boarding house feeling that he might have, at last, reached the bend in the river, that this could be the juncture where his past could finally be wrapped in delicate tissues and treasured as a memory. It would be best after all if he did not return, he had reasoned, if he did not return to Calcutta for a very long time, for a very long time. But he had woken the following morning with a merciless throbbing in his temples, and a stale taste in his mouth which lingered through the day, and Amira catching up with him after a lecture had explained that it was probably the effect of the excess of wine, and suggested that they nip into the Kings Arms to treat poison with poison, a pint of cider she seemed to feel might cure him. He had taken her advice and consumed not one pint but three, after which they had walked in the University Parks until dusk, which did not happen till late, for it was almost the end of May. At the duckpond, she had produced from her handbag a few slices of bread and watching her tear them meticulously into even portions for the birds, he had suddenly felt a strange irritation, and then as she became increasingly absorbed in distributing them among the ducks so that none might receive less than another, he had started to wish that he was not with her at all, and closing his eyes he had imagined in much detail how it would be to be there with Reba, tracing in his mind's eye the curve of her elbow as she might fling the food to the ducks, the deliciously random arc of her throw that would confirm for him that her pleasure was in the act of feeding them rather than making sure that each received its fair share. Amira turned towards him in the light of the setting sun, she was so beautiful it took his breath away, and yet he could only take her hand like a stranger's to shake in farewell. It was wonderful to walk with you in the park, he said.

Jennifer was waiting for him in the sitting room when he returned to the boarding house. You have missed supper, she reminded him, but I can make you some sandwiches if you like. Her aunt had already gone to bed.

No, thank you, he said, but come and sit with me awhile.

She was much taken aback by this request, and rose to join him by the window, would you like a glass of port? she asked.

No, thank you, he said.

Is anything wrong? she asked, lifting her large eyes to his face.

He looked at her and smiled, it would be all right, he thought to himself, to feed the ducks with her.

I am marrying an English girl, he wrote to Reba, the following day, *I hope I will have your blessing, as well as that of my elder brother*. He had put it aside before it was finished for he promised to go punting with Amira that afternoon, and was late to meet her.

I am getting married, he told her, as they glided past a branch, her fingers froze upon the bark, for she had reached out to push it away. I am happy to hear that, she said.

For the rest of the trip she lay with her face to the sun, her eyes hidden behind vast sunglasses.

You punt extremely well, she said to him as she stepped out of the boat.

I come from a land of rivers, he replied. I learnt to punt before I could say nursery rhymes. But then, before I was really old enough to remember much of it, we had to leave.

She paused to listen, briefly mesmerized.

I was born on our feudal estate in East Bengal, he explained. Our father had packed us off to the country for fear that the Japanese would bomb Calcutta.

And did they? she asked.

They did, he said, but I lay safe in my ancestral cot, girded by water, far far away.

What a life you have led, she said, rather wistfully.

Yours has been no less a life surely.

Perhaps I cannot tell it the way you do, she said.

For him there was no peace such as that in the dividing of water under one's oar, the scorings of the pole upon the soft waves, the darkness of the sky reflecting upon the surface with the promise of more rain. There is no suffering like the suffering of water, he told Amira, the sadness of a river as it breaches its own banks and engulfs the very lands that it has fed.

That is sad indeed, she said, and taking her sunglasses off, she pierced him for the last time with her lavish liquid gaze, said goodbye and walked away.

Afterwards he walked for a long while by the river, for he knew that the choices were still open to him, that Jennifer would never dare ask whether he really meant to marry her if he never brought it up again, that Amira would accept his explanation that it had been an arranged marriage that he had alluded to, which was probably what she believed anyway, it would not be difficult to tell her that he had decided not to succumb to his father's wishes, if anything it was likely to have the effect of forcing a certain clarity upon their relationship, for it would be implicit that she had been the reason for his withdrawal. The choice was his, and for the first time in his life Debendranath Roy found himself in a state of indecision, the agony of which came not from his caring deeply about either alternative, but that each, in its own way, was permanent. Sitting upon the riverbank and watching the punts and rowboats pass by crowded with happy faces, he felt a certain mellowness, and began to reason that it would not be too bad to stay on in Oxford, take up the offer of studying for a D. Phil, pursue the relationship with Amira, which, although it might lead to nothing, would give him the opportunity to build a life here for himself, a life that was entirely his own, and from the security of this existence he could continue to worship her, to hold her sacred, his brother's wife, Reba, who could never belong to him in any other way. And if this life should consume him, and her place in it dwindle to a mere skein of rich colour, what harm was there in that? For in the three years that he had been at Oxford, he had made no attempt at all to socialize with anyone, had allowed his studies to consume him, had very little contact with humanity other than Jennifer's mild company, and on the occasional insistence of his fellow countrymen to join them for an evening of spiced food and sitar music, he had not allowed himself the liberty of learning to forget Reba, or even let her illuminate his existence obliquely, rather than scorching all his senses to fine dust. It was entirely possible, he told himself, as he hastened back to his lodgings, that he would be able to find a way to treasure her without letting her consume him, and to embark upon this he needed to be apart from her a while longer, a few more years, add some more substance to himself. He should tear up the letter he had written to her earlier that afternoon, and never again allude to marriage with Jennifer, who would hopefully forgive him. But when he stepped into the house, they were waiting with champagne, the landlady and all the boarders, congratulations, they said to him, and taking the glass that was offered to him, Debendranath Roy submitted gratefully to this other fate.

INDIGO

They arrived in Calcutta on a rainy day in July. His father had come to meet them, and with him were his son's children, for a trip to the airport was considered a treat then, it was 1969, and it had been three years since he had made the voyage by sea to distant Oxford. The presence of the children eased the situation, for Jennifer managed to captivate them immediately with tales of their voyage, although they could not understand her accent very well, and had to ask her many times to repeat what she had said. His father, he felt, looked old and tired, and somehow inappropriately dressed in a jacket and tie. He shook hands cordially with Jennifer but spoke resolutely in Bengali throughout the journey home, and Debendranath Roy was glad that she was engaged in a conversation with the children for otherwise it would have been uncomfortably obvious that she was being ignored. His nephews, whom he had left as toddlers, had become proper little boys now, and his niece, Niharika, had grown into something so lovely he could hardly bear to take his eyes away from her as she nestled rather dreamily by his side in the crowded car, not quite as interested as her brothers in their uncle and his new wife, laughing with them when they laughed, but with most of her concentration fisted in its own world of ogresses and flying horses. He noticed with pleasure that there was no bashfulness in her manner towards him. It was as if there had been no discontinuity in their relationship, even though he had left when she was hardly two years old. When the car came to a halt in the portico, she opened the door and dashed out to her mother, who had appeared in one of the doorways. Debendranath Roy descended with his eyes fixed upon the ground, and then he raised them, like two hollow lanterns, towards the woman he loved, framed in the tall doorway with her little daughter clutching the drapes of her sari, he looked upon her as she stood silhouetted in the stormlight and knew that he should never have returned.

A new set of rooms had been prepared for them, and he was glad to be told that he would have the use of his old room as a study, for it was in a quiet corner of the house whereas the suite where they were to live was to the front of the house and rather noisy. Also, the rest of that floor was occupied by the children, who played all day on the broad balcony, when they were not at school. His old rocking horse was still there he noticed, a little more jaded, but still boldly carrying its small passengers to heights of ecstasy upon its chipped back. Once, when they had all been in desperate need of ground red chillies to flavour their slices of raw mango, many many years ago, he had made his sisters place them on a newspaper under the horse, and crushed them under the weight of his rocking, most of them had flown all over the place, but enough was obtained to sprinkle upon their mango slices, with mustard oil and salt, a favourite afternoon treat. The rocking horse was still giving service, he was pleased to see, and his niece seemed to treat it as if it were alive, bringing it water and oatmeal, raided from the larder. They eat oats, don't they, she had asked him, and showed him a book of an English farm. I wish I had a horse, she said.

But you have a squirrel, he pointed out to her, and all those guinea pigs in the cage in the garden.

The guinea pigs belong to my brothers, she said. Besides, they are awfully dull.

The squirrel was officially hers and was allowed to scamper about on the balcony on a very long chain which it had come to accept almost as part of its body. Her mother would not let it come into the house, for Reba cared for animals only at a distance, their proximity disgusted her. She saved the scraps of their meals for stray cats, as she had always done, but she had no use for their affection, would rather die than touch them, and once a mouse running over her bare feet had caused her to shudder so violently that Debendranath Roy had been crushed by the lushness of her displeasure.

She hated too to tread barefoot upon any surface, and he had seen her squirm in agony as her toes were splashed with mud on a monsoon day as she picked way through the puddles upon the cracked pavements. He had seen her recoil in horror from the oily skin of a weedchoked pond as it stretched to fill her sandals while she pleaded with her sons to wade back out. And each time he had feasted on these anxieties, to him they were profoundly sensual, her dislikes seemed more integral to her than her likes, for with the former she had had no choice in the matter. Her daughter seemed not to have inherited this squeamishness which would have got in the way of her passion for all living creatures, so she kept all her treasures hidden from her mother, small spiders in matchboxes, antlion larvae in her pencil box, she once managed to sneak in a stray goatkid that she kept for a whole night under her bed.

Jennifer quickly became her ally in collecting and maintaining her secret menagerie. Together they followed the strange routine of the dung beetles in their garden, released tadpoles into the ornamental pond to watch them grow into frogs, sheltered injured strays in the gatekeeper's shed. Jennifer was a farmer's daughter and knew how to tend to their wounds. And often Debendranath Roy would watch her as she stood silently by while Reba scolded her daughter for these misdemeanours, smiling awkwardly as her own humiliation mounted, but never daring to defend the child. He would watch her slowly twisting her limp hair between her fingers and in an odd way, he would feel proud of his wife that she never felt the need to assert herself in these situations, that she could quietly accept her role as an accessory without entirely losing her dignity.

Indeed, in the years that they spent together, after they left Calcutta, and before he drowned in the Cherwell, he was always grateful to her for gently illuminating his existence with her humility. He who had accepted darkness as his only path

35

would sit with her upon the stone steps of a marvellous cathedral on their many travels, and feel a deep satisfaction in the shape of his life, that she should be at his side, a soothing presence, while the rest of him was immersed in the contemplation of the woman whom he so desperately wanted there with him, wanted there beside him upon the cathedral steps, biting her lips perhaps as she reread the guide book, wanted there with him inside the velvet holiness of the cathedral transepts, her face streaked with the blue of old stained glass, wanted with him afterwards there across the table from him as they lunched on mussels and straw chips, wanted with him so badly that he could only be grateful to Jennifer that to have her with him instead did not create within him an impossible disharmony, that he was able to take pleasure instead in her innocent delight in everything, kiss away her tears when she felt she might have displeased him in any way.

And yet, even this, in the end, was not enough, for one warm spring day, five years after they had returned to England, he took the train to Oxford to see one of his old professors about the possibility of returning to academia, of embarking once more on the course of research that he had plotted out for himself while he had been a student there. It was too early in the year yet for tourists, and walking back to the railway station, he was suddenly seized with the desire to spend a few quiet moments on the river. He hired a punt and moved off, glided for a while upon the turbid waters, and then finding a quiet spot, pulled up against the shore. He stretched back and closed his eyes and let in the same shadows, and found them suddenly too heavy for his widemeshed thoughts, memories fell through him like pieces of tarnished cutlery, he opened his eyes and realized that he was too full of holes to return to this world.

He remembered her as he had first seen her when they had assembled in the booklined drawing room of her father's flat to inspect her as a possible wife for his brother. He had been studying for his Intermediate examinations at the time, and had been reluctant to join the party, besides, the whole concept was revolting to him, to appraise a woman in this manner. He had passed no judgement upon her, indeed he had not formed an impression of her, except that she radiated a certain dignity, for which he felt mildly grateful, since it had made it impossible for anyone to be condescending with her, which was the usual tone of these transactions. The wedding he hardly remembered for the horrible heat, and how he had attempted to entertain the various children of his three sisters, and keep them from wandering too close to the pond beside the grand marquee. He had returned, exhausted and resentful of having relinquished an evening of quiet study for this ill-timed event, and passed the night in fruitless battle with a wily mosquito that had crept inside his bednet. In the morning he had caught it clinging upside down from the roof of the net, its belly full of his blood. That evening, the new bride had arrived with her husband, and he had watched in bemused silence as the women gathered around her, blew their conch shells, and gave her a fish to hold upon a platter as she entered her new home. At the threshold she tipped a vessel of rice with a decorated toe, and stepped into a bowl of milk, and as his eldest sister stooped to ritualistically wipe her feet with her hair, Debendranath Roy had felt a curious chill in how regally she appeared to accept this gesture. He had watched his mother daub the new bride's lips with honey so that none but sweet words would ever issue from them, and had been filled with an aching anger that Reba would someday take her place as mistress of this house. Why must things change at all? he had wondered, turning his eyes from the joyous proceedings towards the sky outside, where the April clouds were gathering to drown the night in lashing rain.

He saw very little of her in the first days of her marriage, preoccupied as he was with his studies, and she with her new role as the wife of the eldest son of a grand and rich family. She herself came from a family of much refinement but of moderate means, a family that had lost much of its fortune during the War and the Partition of Bengal, but whose wealth, when it had been, was old and solid, stretching far back into the meshes of the under-recorded history of Bengal, while his father had made his money only this century in Burma teak.

She came from a family of gifted musicians, a family whose talents had flowed in their veins through many generations like a suspension of gold dust, washed by time into a thin but brilliant stream. Every day she would wake at dawn to practise upon her *esraj*, at about the same time that Debendranath Roy would rise to return to his books, for it was in these early hours that he was most able to concentrate on the intricacies of the physical universe, to appreciate its symmetries, to internalize its rhythms so skillfully coded in the language of mathematics. He found the music distracting at first, her strange communion with the instrument, now wounding now caressing, but always mournful. He found it hard to digest his calculus while she practised on her *esraj*, and one morning he decided to tell her so.

He came and stood behind the curtain of her bedroom door, cleared his throat and knocked lightly. She did not hear him. He moved the curtain a fraction with his finger, saw her face in profile, her long hair cascading over an arched shoulder, her gaze fixed towards a deadly distant point. He saw her in this state of terrible rigid perfection, and quickly dropped the curtain, returned to his desk, and sat for a while, his heart pounding, his head throbbing, until quite suddenly a trespasser's lightness came to trip through his senses, he blew upon a cobweb that stretched between his desklamp and the bookshelf, and caught the falling clot of threads in his palm.

He was young then, so very young, and he had found it easier to despise her than to try and understand her, to blame her for his mother's strange madness. For three years and more he hardly ever spoke to Reba, never did he imagine that part of her soul was famished within the great house where she was mistress, never once did he see her loneliness, the desperate loneliness that later he would find almost too beautiful to behold. He did not know how she ached at times to run back home, to rest her head upon familiar old floor cushions and listen to music or argue with her father, the venerable Professor of Ancient Indian History. Her father must have missed her dreadfully too, although it was not as if he was ever alone, many of his old students still visited him regularly, brought their students to meet him, and unless he visited in those stealthy silent afternoon hours following lunch, Debendranath Roy was sure to find himself in the midst of an animated group discussion, the Professor moderating between his many acolytes. For it had quickly become a habit with him to make his way after college, or even in between classes, to the Professor's home – long after Reba had come home with the children, Debendranath Roy found himself regularly drawn to these sessions. Tall and hollow-cheeked, his figure emaciated like a sketch rubbed out and refined one too many a time, the Professor always spoke with utmost precision, choosing his words with relish, and never allowing an English expression to slip in except under the heavy harness of quotation marks which he would signify with a vibrato of his slender fingers. Debendranath Roy had never met anyone like him, his own family seemed hopelessly uncultivated by contrast. Why had he agreed to give his only daughter in marriage to them, he had wondered, was it simply their wealth, did he simply wish to deliver his daughter from the anxieties that he had endured in his own life, watching his family fortunes wither, finding himself having to think twice before purchasing a book, restringing an instrument, ordering tiger prawns for a nephew's birthday feast. Or perhaps he had simply succumbed to the will of his wife, so long in her sickroom, wishing to see her daughter securely married. Indeed, her health had improved dramatically since Debendranath Roy had first seen her, ghostly pale beside her daughter, when they had arrived to examine Reba as a candidate for the hallowed position of his brother's wife. There was something strongly feminine about her then, something deep and lush in the dark circles of

39

her eyes, something frail and cold in her invalid hands, something that had been replaced after her daughter's marriage by a neutral warmth, a genderless sense of well-being. She was often to be seen afterwards reading in her rocking chair upon the small balcony outside her room, or knitting small garments for her grandchildren, sometimes she would even ask the maid to bring her a vessel of water and a ladle so that she might water the potted plants that Reba had so lovingly arranged there many years ago. When he heard, in his second year in Oxford, that she had suddenly died, he had tried to conceive of the quality of Reba's grief at the loss of a mother who only came to life after she had left home, but like so much else within her he had found it impossible to imagine.

He remembered how Reba's mother would draw him aside from the crowd of young men at her husband's feet, beckon him to follow her into the dining room where she would offer him some delicate sweetmeat or a fried piece of the fish they had had for lunch, if it was especially fresh. Do eat, she would coax, unfortunately I do not have enough for everybody out there. Though that very thought was ridiculous, since so many people trooped in and out of the flat from late afternoon until late evening, and maids' hands became sore with serving tea. The first time that he returned from an evening of violent emotional discourse at the Professor's flat, he felt almost embarassed to tell Reba that he had been there in her absence, and even later, when it became an established habit, he would sense within her a certain contempt towards his addiction to the society of these young and earnest intellectuals. It was as if she felt, had always felt, that she was superior to them, the young men that crowded about her father's feet, it was clear she did not want to see him as just one of them. For something else had begun to take shape between them, he did not yet know quite what it was, just an overwhelming urge to save every thought he had to tell her later, to note every strange thing he saw for her amusement, to share the beauty of all he read, even the equations that described the laws of the universe he felt he could explain to her, if she had the inclination to listen. But he never dared to ask her if she would afford him the pleasure of acquainting her with the strange metaphors that men had constructed to rationalize the mystery of the stars without wringing it of its wonder, occasionally he would tempt her with poetic conundrums – they say the stars in the universe are older than the universe itself – he would tell her, but she never once responded with how can that be true? – she would smile, and acknowledge the profundity of such a concept, and her smiles would fall into him like rain falling after drought into the cupped palms of an aceramic race.

And Indranath Roy, watching his son change and grow more distant every day, felt that he had lost him, not to Reba, but to her father, the old professor in his dusty flat, from whom he had taken a most beloved daughter. It was as if this was his revenge, to take from him his younger son, tutor him in all sorts of political blasphemy, turn his mind with poetry and sad rainsong. The boy had always been so susceptible, unlike his other children, the boy had a strange quality of restlessness, and yet it was this child that he loved most, for in him he saw something of his dead wife, so brutally absent in all the other children she had borne him. They had come so easily into this world, as if blown off her like the whiskers of a dandelion, while Debendranath's birth had almost killed her, she had been seized by a deathly fever, and although she recovered, was pale and weak for many months afterward, and so serene in her illness that Indranath Roy felt it would be obscene to touch her, except perhaps to caress her forehead, and by degrees it became too remote a possibility that his devotion to her might once have been flecked with lust. Just to interrupt her in her daily routine came to have for him the sensation of tearing through gauze, to ask her to lift her lovely eyes from the book she might be reading or from her embroidery came to feel like an act of far greater violence than all the transactions of his timber business, which had, after the War and Independence, begun to shrink at a rate that he might have found alarming, if he had not known that even if it were to collapse into nothing, he would still be able to give her and his children the life that he felt they deserved.

And yet it had been enough to him that his life had been graced by her presence, that he might peep out of his office window at some pause within the day's business and be presented with the comforting spectacle of her, sitting in the shade of the magnolia trees, her infant son resting in her arms, their older son lying beside her, absorbed in his storybook, and the three girls gambolling upon the lawn within the firm embrace of familiar childhood chants, their small secrets tumbling about them, his daughters, who seemed to him later to have simply swept like elven lights through their household, slender little things always in each other's embrace, they had been given early in marriage to appropriate men, all three of them, and had made their own charming, inconsequential lives within the narrow and select social circles that he had forced them to inhabit, had beautiful children of their own that would crowd about him on feast days like flowers, and eventually almost all emigrated to far away, affluent lands.

Indeed, more ravishing than ever was she in her languid withdrawal from the world around her, he had thought of his wife, his eyes resting upon her long fingers calm upon the brow of their youngest daughter quaking with measles in the heat of the endless afternoon. The stillness of her vigil had stirred within him an almost delicious disquiet, that same longing to possess and enshrine her that had gripped him many years ago when he had spotted her walking back from school in a small North Bengal town, regal in unbleached homespun, a thick black braid falling across the pale arch of her shoulder, who is she? he had asked the mill manager, the young girl with the books, who is she?

After her death, he found he could no longer inhabit their bedchamber, and ordered them to place a single bed in a small room adjoining his vast study, and there he slept, in his monastic quarters, his tobacco pipe and flask of water beside him, and his wristwatch, which he would let his grandchildren wind, if they ran some small errand for him to earn the privilege. He found it hard to return at night to the room where she had died, for in the dark he would feel often that he might reach over and find her kneeling against the bed, weeping into the heavy covers, her hair coiled into a tight bun against her neck, as he had found her on the day that she was to have sat in private for her Matriculation exams, a few months after they were married. The evening before, as she fanned him during his meal, she had asked him timidly whether he was aware that she was meant to sit for her examinations the next day, had any arrangements been made to convey her to the examination hall? He had smiled and promised to send a car for her at eight o'clock, for the first paper was at nine o'clock, in English Literature, followed that afternoon by English Language. Strange that they should put Literature before Language, he had commented, digging into his cauliflower curry.

On that day, she woke at dawn with a tinny sense of the unreal, she bathed carefully, and gathered flowers for her morning prayers, helped her husband prepare himself for his journey to their mills north of the city. She tried to coax herself to remind him of the car to take her to the examination hall, but no sooner had she gathered the courage to bring it up than it would drain away, every time. But as he was leaving, Indranath Roy touched his wife's arm, the car will come for you at eight, he told her. Do not panic, and do the best you can, he said, filling her with relief and gladness. She returned to her room, and quietly flicked through her grammar notes, her heart sounding within her like a distant but heavy gong. And precisely at eight o'clock, a car horn sounded outside. She gathered her books and pencil case, and came down the stairs, through the swing doors, and was about to put on her sandals, when she thought she should ask her mother-in-law's blessing before she left, for she had never left the house before without

43

doing so, and this, of all occasions, merited a blessing, this, of all occasions, demanded that she not steal away like a sorry thief, this holy act of appearing as a private candidate for her Matriculation exams.

She found her mother-in-law seated on the dining room floor, rolling dough, and this to her did not auger well, for such things were usually left to the cook and his bevy of kitchenmates, a dark clot of fear rose in her throat as she knelt to touch the older woman's floury feet.

If you are going to the Kalighat temples, be sure to bring back some vermilion, her mother-in-law said to her.

Later, it struck her that she might have simply nodded and left, and all would have been well, but instead she told her that she was going to sit for her exams, as she had been promised when they had demanded her as a bride, six months ago, for their son.

Oh, but you cannot do that today, her mother-in-law said.

She gazed in horror upon the bowed head, the corpulent lips from which these words came, the hands rolling dough into small flat circles of pale white.

You cannot go today, her mother-in-law repeated. She was told that a distant but important elderly relation was coming to spend the day, coming all the way from Chinsurah to see her, for he had been too ill to come to the wedding, he was expected any minute, it would not do for her to be absent for the whole day.

Later, she cursed herself for having come to ask her blessings at all, but knew all the time that it would not have made a difference, for even if she had managed to sneak away on that day, the day after she would surely have been somehow detained, and if not the day after then the day after the day after, she locked herself in the bathroom and sobbed bitterly for as long as she was able to stay unnoticed in there. That night, she lay restless by her husband's side, for he had consoled her with the thought that she might be able to take them the following year. Things will be more settled then, he had reassured her, you will have become more accustomed to this life, and perhaps be in a better frame of mind to take on such a challenge. I will engage tutors for you, he had promised her, so that you will be better prepared. Meanwhile he would speak to his mother, he said, so that she would come to understand how important it was for his wife to continue her education. You must forgive her, he told her, she is from another time, another age, she has no notion of why women might want to know more than how to read and write and do their accounts.

You can sit for your Matriculation next year, he told her, but when next year came she was heavily pregnant, and looking forward only to going back to her parents to have the child. It was a son and everyone was very pleased with her, her husband even asked her if she wanted him to arrange for her to take her exams that summer, but she shook her head, perhaps next year, when the child is older, she said. And then it happened that the world seemed to separate itself from her, that all her worries and concerns seemed suddenly to touch her upon the shoulder sadly and leave, the War came, and she realized she did not care whether humanity redeemed itself or not, she who had once vowed to devote her life to the struggle to free her country from the yoke of imperialism, now felt that the fate of the world was of no consequence to her at all. Three daughters were born to her, and then another son, Debendranath, born to her in the depths of disaster, of flood, famine and starvation. She contracted a deathly fever upon his birth, and when it retreated it took with it all traces of yearning, and she felt a deep consummate peace, unearthly and unkind, which she knew would sustain her for the rest of her life.

This was the great stillness that Debendranath Roy knew, like the silence within a dark and broken temple, soft with stale sandalwood. He had never thought that it might be corrupted simply by another woman coming into their midst and quietly transforming her corner of the house. He had been apprehensive, but more for the woman who would come into their

45

household as his brother's wife, for he knew that while both he and his brother adored their mother, his sisters found her cold and distant. He had been worried that his sister-in-law might feel the same. In fact he never found out what Reba thought of his mother, though at the time he had imagined that she was amused that the older woman was so desperately trying to emulate her, and although now he knew that this was not true, he also knew that she never blamed herself, as many others would have, for her mother-in-law's madness. She may have exacerbated or even been entirely responsible for the symptoms, but she knew she was not the cause. No, the reasons for her madness lay lost deep in time. Once, going through a trunkful of old saris, Reba had found two old algebra and geometry texts, scored and scribbled over in a woman's hand that she surmised must have been her mother-in-law's. Reba had brought them to him, the battered little books that had belonged so many years ago to his mother, she had brought them to him while he sat at his desk studying for his final examinations, I found these in an old trunk, she had said, I thought you might like to have them. And holding them in his hands, he remembered her as she guided them through their homework, quiet and clear, gently pointing out their mistakes not so much by words as by simply repeating the exercise correctly, and sometimes she would pause and show them, as it suddenly came to her, a more elegant way of solving the problem, and sigh, as if in doing so, she might have caught a glimpse of the rich tapestry of a future that was denied to her.

Sometimes he wondered what his mother would have thought of Jennifer, and always he felt that she would have liked her, that she would have warmed to the simple sweetness of her soul, her honesty, her humility, for somewhere within it all was a desire to make of life a little more than what it appeared to offer her. From the correspondence course in librarianship to her weekly attendance at lectures on world religions, he saw, like crocuses scattered gently upon a tired lawn, fragments everywhere of a desire to make of herself a little more than what it was obvious she could be. He felt that his mother would have liked her, even when he found it so hard himself to love her as he should, as she shifted and stirred in her sleep beside him, upon the great bed that had once belonged to his grandparents. The heat had taken the apple-sweet crispness out of her features, her brown hair fell upon her shoulders in a loose lank mass. The tropics did not suit her, and although the thick walls of their house shielded her somewhat from the heat, she wilted from the humidity, the hot August nights stamped through her like herds of panting buffalo, and she woke feeling more drained and tired than when she had come to bed, dreading the rest of the day.

Your wife does not seem very healthy, his father observed.

Who would be? Debendranath Roy retorted. Who would not be ill encountering this heat for the first time?

I have known many Englishwomen in my time, his father replied, and it always seemed to me that they had a remarkable capacity for enduring the heat. I would always marvel at how fresh and cool they looked even when it was most beastly hot outside. Of course in those days women were more anxious to appear composed.

I am sorry that my wife is not reacting to the heat appropriately, said Debendranath Roy.

Why must you make the worst of everything I say? asked his father.

I wish I knew how to put some other complexion on it, he replied.

Relations with his father had been strained since he had returned with his English wife to Calcutta, for his father had found it hard to hide his disappointment that she was not, by his standards, at all pretty, and more so that she had such little education. Whether it mattered greatly to him that she was not of their race, Debendranath Roy could not fathom, but it was clear that it was less of a consideration than her qualities. And even more than this, his father was disappointed that he had come back home at all, rather than staying on to do a D. Phil.

47

It had always seemed to him that this younger son of his should become an academic, it was what his mother would have wished, Indranath Roy had reasoned, and he had set aside a chunk of his fortune for this very purpose. And here he was now, paused in a state of supreme indecision, and burdened with a talentless wife, with whom he was already disenchanted, and this was what troubled him most, more than his inherent disapproval of her. It hurt him deeply that his son would spend the rest of his life with a woman that he did not utterly adore, as he had adored his own wife, even though he had never been able to make her happy. Now she was gone, his only route to any kind of happiness was to believe that he had achieved something she would have desired, like sending Debendranath to Oxford, setting him up so that he could dedicate the rest of his life to unravelling the mysteries of the universe, unhampered by financial worries, the terrible need to feed and clothe and provide a future for those that he most loved. And instead, here he was, in Calcutta again, although it was not clear that he was wasting his time, for he would leave soon after breakfast to go and sit in a library until lunchtime, after a late lunch he would read at home, locked in his study, and then he would slip away, to see his friends, or to stop by at Reba's father's flat where his students still congregated daily, and then after dinner he would lock himself up in his study again. Often, Indranath Roy would hope that he would perhaps approach him with a plan already substantiated, or better still a scheme where his father could assist his progress, for nothing would have pleased him better than to still play a large part in his life.

Will you talk to him? Indranath Roy asked Reba, he always listens to you.

I will, she promised, and later that week, she found him, on the large balcony looking out onto the garden where he had spent his afternoons as a child in the shade of the fig trees with his mother, his sisters chattering together in a tight magpie knot just out of earshot, and his brother stretched out on the grass doing his homework or reading detective stories. She found him gazing into the greenness, made dull by the smoke-smothered sunlight. They were alone in the house, except for the servants, for Jennifer had taken the children to the cinema, and his father and brother were visiting a mill several miles north of the city.

For a while they stood silently, watching a little girl playing with her dog on the roof terrace of a house across the road.

You promised once to tell me, she said, what makes the earth go round the sun.

He made a sound that was somewhere between a laugh and a sigh.

Why this? he asked. Why now?

Just something that I remembered, she said.

And did I ever explain to you why the earth goes round the sun?

No, she said. And I am not even sure that it does, she said with a small laugh.

What makes you say that? he asked.

What proof have I that it does, beyond that I have been told it is so?

Would it please you more to believe that you are at the centre of the universe, and everything else revolves around you?

No, that would be too great a burden.

Too great a burden for whom?

For humanity, of course.

And why is it a burden to know that you are the focus of everything, the one immutable absolute, around which everything else must arrange itself?

If it had not been such a burden, why were we so keen to eschew such a notion, and replace it with our utter insignificance?

There is more mystery in insignificance, he replied.

And are these our only choices? she asked. To be everything or nothing? Is there nothing in between?

Nothing of any value, he said, looking suddenly, for the first time in his life with meaning, into her eyes. Talk to me sometimes, will you, talk to me sometimes like this, he said.

She looked down upon her hands sternly gripping the balcony rail, and in the hardribbed white of her knuckles she saw how desperately she had tried to squeeze him into the cast of a young brother-in-law, interpret the quality of his misery as youthful irresolution, how hard she had tried to dismiss his obvious despair as the bitter aftertaste of a hasty, unfortunate marriage. She looked down between the balcony rails at the ornamental pond below, enamelled with balsam blossoms, and realized that it was not for any of these reasons that he was planning to do nothing, absolutely nothing with life.

She looked up again and saw him as he stood staring into the grim distance, his mouth pressed into a thin sharp line of pain, and she was glad of the grandeur of his desolation, for in the past few months she had felt nothing but contempt for him and his unhappy wife. She had found it hard to see him in Jennifer's company for she felt that there was so little between them, and yet would it not have been harder, she had sometimes contemplated, if he had returned with a glamorous European princess, or harder still if he had found a Bengali woman in Oxford, in every respect his peer, with whom he might have shared his life more fully than he could ever have done with her. But no, it would have been easier, she had reasoned, for with a woman that she could respect, a certain companionship would have evolved, a certain collusion, and some part of his satisfaction in his relationship with his wife would have cemented around his regard for her, which perhaps then could have been nurtured simply as a deep regard, once tinged with a youthful passion, for his elder brother's wife. But looking at him now, she saw that this would not have been what he would have wanted, it would never have been enough for him to shelter her as a divine memory, to allow his emotions towards her to swell and be consumed by a solid and abiding respect. She saw that he would rather live in the conviction that nothing in his life was better than her, even as she was, inaccessible, unpossessable, utterly outside all his boundaries. She looked into his eyes and then, without saying another word she turned and left, left him looking down upon the tired lawn where he had played as a child. And for the first time since he had loved her, he felt that he had finally seen what for so long he had been trying to see, like a mirror in the dark. He had waited for a very long time for that small flicker of light that would betray its presence, and now that it had come, he knew he must leave.

In the depths of which dream did you place upon my
   neck
this garland of love, this garland of pain?
I woke and found among the red clouds of dawn
the flute strains of our farewell.
For you had come and gone in silence,
and bound me, while I slept, in chords of awful
   darkness
clad me unawares in the sublime anguish of loss.
In the depths of which dream did you pass,
leaving around my neck this precious garland of pain?

They had been in Calcutta for almost a whole year now, and it had not been unpleasant. The heat bothered Jennifer terribly, and in the winter the smog irritated her lungs, but in her state of sickliness, she was easy to feel affection for, easy to soothe, and her determination to adjust to the climate, not to mention her strange new existence, was often intensely touching to Debendranath Roy. She was devoted to the children, and managed to fill her days with them, fetching them from school, bathing them, and thinking up things for them to do when it was raining outside and they had read all their storybooks. He knew that she thought their mother neglected them, for Reba seemed to be permanently occupied with her music. She had started giving professional recitals, it took up a lot of her time.

He did not know whether her children felt that she was no longer there for them, but he certainly felt that he had lost her to this passion, that since he had left it had risen to consume her, and he could only dare hope that it was the void that his absence had created that had spurred this calamity. But what was there left for him to do anyway besides sit among his books and dream of how it had been once, and for a year this was what he had happily done, until the fateful afternoon when she had approached him, as a favour to her father-in-law, to ask him what he meant to do with the rest of his life, and the old harmony had broken through, as if waiting strenuously to fill the chasm between them, except that it had been clear to both of them that this was no longer just a haunting melody, but the abiding rhythm of his life.

He felt more keenly than ever that he had failed her, failed her in his lack of commitment to his studies, failed her by making no attempt to forget her even though this would cripple his existence forever, failed her in choosing to be content with such an ordinary wife. He remembered a frivolous conversation they had had, on the day before he had first left for Oxford. They were sitting on the balcony as usual, he was playing Ludo with her sons, she was sewing buttons onto the shirts he would pack that evening into the great trunk that he was taking with him on his long voyage. And suddenly she asked him – if you married an English girl, what would we call her?

He turned the volume down on the radio, what do you mean, he asked, what would we call her?

Oh, we could never call her by her English name, she said playfully, we would have to find a Bengali name for her.

You seem to have already invented her, he replied.

Take these, she said, putting a glass needlecase into his hand, I doubt whether your landlady will sew your missing buttons on for you.

What about my English girl? he asked. Won't she sew my buttons?

None of the English girls I went to school with had the least idea of how to sew a button.

But these were the daughters of wealthy colonials, he retorted. I understand that most people in England don't even have servants.

If you marry an English girl, said Reba, surely she will at least be a noblewoman, perhaps even a countess.

You have certainly already invented her, said Debendranath Roy.

I am marrying an English girl, he had written to her, *she is my landlady's niece, she is a simple country girl, I think you will like her*. And indeed, he never felt in the time that they lived together in Calcutta that Reba's manner towards his wife was ever tinged with any dislike, sometimes he felt that she treated her as she might have treated a daughter that he had brought back to India after her mother had died or run away, with a sort of deliberate kindness, but not without affection. Jennifer, like everyone else, was in complete awe of her, but unlike many others she accepted her intimidation with grace, and there was no disharmony between them. There was no disharmony indeed in anything else, except for his relationship with his father, who found it hard to tolerate his dreaminess, the depth of his inaction, his complete lack of purpose, that fit so easily in with the schedules of all the other members of the household. His brother, entirely absorbed in the family business, was happy that he was back in the house, happy to believe that he was committed to his studies, happy to see him at the dinner table and discuss politics and ask him questions about his time in England. His brother was perhaps the only one of them who was pleased that he had married Jennifer, so sweetly submissive, you would have to look hard these days to find a Bengali wife who was so concerned with your happiness, he told Debendranath Roy.

And the children seem to adore her, he added with

something of a sigh. Which is just as well, because their mother seems so preoccupied these days with her music, he said.

They could certainly have carried on like this, each with their own passion, Reba – her music, Jennifer – the children, his brother – the family business, and Debendranath Roy immersed in the contemplation of her loneliness, it was clearer than ever to him now, as she played for hours upon the *esraj* behind tightly shut doors, rushed between rehearsals, and sat at mealtimes, now no longer hooded by her sari, but enshrouded instead by her almost morbid dedication to her art. She never cooked anymore in her small kitchen. He remembered how for the twins' fourth birthday she had made two cakes in the shape of two eyes, with candles burning in their irises, and these she had laid upon a large bell metal platter with a string of dark sweetmeats for a smile, and a tomato for a nose, but now she was not to be seen any longer fiddling about with her little blue stove, or polishing the chrome handles of her tiny oven, a birthday present from her father-in-law, which she had once valued almost as much as her musical instruments. Instead, Jennifer would use the little kitchen sometimes, to make fairy cakes and biscuits with little Niharika, which they would offer to Reba when she returned exhausted from her rehearsals. These would be some of their best times together, held in the mellow recognition that this was perhaps exactly as things should be, that Reba should entrust her children to the care of their loving aunt, while she pursued her true calling, that each was doing what they were best at and what they best liked to do. And then the spell would be broken as Reba would wearily rise and set about rearranging the shelves which they had tried to leave in order but had once again failed to, and Jennifer would apologize, and the child would take her cookies to her grandfather or her uncle, where they were sure to be unconditionally appreciated.

She was an unusual child, and Debendranath Roy could not often help but feel that she was destined for something quite beyond what was possible for any of the rest of them. She was of course intelligent and creative, but no more so than her brothers, and at times she seemed almost a little slow, hopelessly gullible, but this he interpreted not as a sign of her stupidity, but as proof that she had not closed her mind to any wealth of possibilities. If you told her that mice ate cheese omelettes for breakfast, she would believe you, but only because it let her small mind travel in a new and exciting direction, and this pleased him more than he could say. He took her once with him to the Planetarium, only a short walk away from their house, for Jennifer was unwell, and the child had complained all day about her being in bed. They sat in the cool darkness in an almost empty hall, for it was not a time when it was likely to be crowded, and then the heavens opened above them, and they were lost in the massive movements of the stars and the comets and the rush of the galaxies, spinning away into infinity. He held her small hand as she sat transfixed, engulfed within the stretches of dark velvet time, unfolding like a liquid within another lighter liquid before her eyes, and he found his mind was spinning with the ecstasy of her perception of the universe, and he knew he had not been so happy in a very long time, not since he had stumbled upon her mother singing in the afternoon stillness, just a few weeks after she was born, singing of the devotee who knew not how to adore the Lord Buddha except through dance:

Every thought of you fills me with the nectar of dance
For this I ask your forgiveness
Every atom of mine quivers in the chant of your grace
As I am steeped in the rhythm of a new birth
Every gesture of mine, every song, has become a
    prayer to you
For this I crave your forgiveness
I tremble with an exquisite pain, dark waves rise
    within me,
As your beauty destroys my calm
Every fragment of my being, and my pain, strives to

rise in prayer towards you
And I beg that my song will not die of shame at your
feet
For my life has been blessed neither by flower or fruit,
My pitcher is empty
For I have not filled it with the water of any
pilgrimage
It is only with your music that my limbs stream
It is only your music that spills from my heart
For this, I ask your forgiveness.

And years later as he lay in his long boat upon the Cherwell, it was this song that gave him the strength to decide once and for all not to return, that the sweet web of lies that was his life had become too distended to contain his love for her. The punt came back without him, and the world was given to know that he was drowned, but Jennifer huddled with grief upon the bathroom floor, raised her eyes to the mirror, saw the streaks still there that he always left from impatiently rubbing off the steam, and could not believe that although these marks were there he was not. It was so unlikely that a swimmer as skillful as he could have met with an accident, and yet she could not bring herself to believe that he might have taken his own life, he had shown no signs of great anguish or despair in the weeks preceding his vanishing, it had in fact been a period of particular tenderness between them. The weather had been unusually beautiful in this late Easter vacation, and they had eaten many of their lunches on Hampstead Heath, she had faithfully followed him around a number of exhibitions that he had appeared to enjoy immensely. How hard it was to think that she would never have the pleasure again of watching him as he stepped back from a painting or a collage with that strange look of intense concentration upon his face, and she would hold her breath as he performed his assessment as if it were her value that was at stake, and then he would look at her and smile, pull her close and kiss her, and sometimes he would tell her why he liked the work and sometimes he would not, and she would listen happily, knowing that it did not matter either to him or to her that she might not understand. It did not seem possible to her that he could have walked away from this and decided in the sweetness of an afternoon to take his life, or that he might have through some act of carelessness let himself drown. She would rather have believed that like Alice he had been seduced by some large white rabbit into Wonderland, or that he had crawled unawares into some magic trunk that had transported him into another world. She could believe that he had left her, but not to lie weedchoked in the depths of the Cherwell. For that he had not been ready, not yet. Perhaps, like the woman in the Tagore story he had recounted to her, he would return and drown again, to prove that he had not drowned before.

After the tragedy, she went back to live with her aunt, and eventually inherited the boarding house which she converted into a Bed & Breakfast, and every evening she would walk out to the Cherwell, and sit upon its banks, and contemplate the thousand shapes of his death. His brother came to see her once, for he passed through London often, and on one occasion he had taken the train up to Oxford, held her hand as she sobbed and sobbed, until her aunt had come in with biscuits and tea. After that, he would always telephone from his hotel but he never visited again. From him she heard that the twin boys had done exceptionally well in their school leaving examinations, that one had gone into medicine and the other into engineering, and then later that they had moved to Delhi and Bombay to pursue their brilliant careers, that one of them had married young and was already a father. She heard that their daughter Niharika had not done as well in school as her brothers, but had nonetheless been offered a place in one of the best colleges to study History – not a competitive subject, her father had explained – but then her performance had improved dramatically, and she had come away with First Class degrees in both her Bachelors and Masters courses. It made Jennifer proud to hear of her achievements, and occasionally she would send her a little card to say so, and always a polite letter arrived to thank her for it, that would hum within her all day as she carried it around in her pocket. And then one day the letter arrived that made her cry with joy, and ring her few friends immediately to tell them that her beloved Niharika was to come to Oxford, like her uncle, to study at the university, it had been seventeen years since she had last seen her, how would she be, she wondered, should she offer to let her live with her, as she so much hoped she would, but her friends told her that a girl of twenty-three will want to live on her own or with friends, not with a middle-aged aunt in a B&B near the railway station. But she suggested it to them anyway, and tried not to be disappointed when her father wrote back to say that the college had already made arrangements for her accommodation, for he also said how deeply reassuring her presence in Oxford was to them, and how he and his wife were sure to take advantage of her hospitality in the next few years. She tried to imagine what she would look like, and realized suddenly that she had never asked for any photographs of them since they had left Calcutta. There had been no communication at all until after her husband had disappeared into the Cherwell, and then she had never thought to ask for any photographs, it had been as if all real links with that episode in her past had been severed. She had never thought that they might be part of her life again.

She remembered how agonizing it had been to leave at her husband's command without bidding anybody farewell, but most especially not to see Niharika for one last time. She had promised to take her to the zoo that day, and to think that she would wake and find her gone forever crippled her with pain. For many months afterwards she wished she had had the nerve to rush into her room and shake her awake to kiss her goodbye, to tell her that she would always love her, no matter where she was, and how many children she might have herself, for she expected that in due course they would have children.

She wished that she had had the courage to wake the child and cover her with kisses. She could not bear to think that Niharika would come to find her as she did every day as soon as her face was washed and her teeth were brushed and she had gulped down her tumbler of morning milk, she would come to knock on her door and find it gaping open, the wardrobes empty and the row of shoes under the windowsill vanished, she thought of how the small feet would drag themselves away in disbelief, and wished that some other pain would come to relieve her of this anguish. In London, she bought books and toys that she felt there would be some way to send her, but Debendranath Roy was adamant that no attempts should be made at reconciliation. She found his resolve all the more frightening because there did not appear to be much anger in him, only a cold rigid determination she did not know how to make sense of. It had all come so suddenly, being shaken awake by him and told to pack. Why? why? she had asked. He had quarrelled with his father, he told her, and she did not dare ask about what. It had been a particularly pleasant evening with his brother telling stories of their boyish exploits upon their country estate, which he remembered vividly while Debendranath Roy remembered only fragments here and there. She had listened happily as he pieced his memories together against the unbroken thread of his brother's recollections, with their father interjecting occasionally, sometimes in English like the rest of them so that she would not feel left out, but more often in Bengali, for he never felt he had to make any concessions for her. She had excused herself early as she had some sewing to do, left them to their memories of mad aunts and thieving monkeys. She never imagined that such an evening could have ended this way.

Debendranath Roy smiled at her as she left, for he had explained to her that it would be most improper for her to kiss him goodnight. Do you not remember the elephant? his brother asked, surely you remember the elephant?

But Debendranath Roy had no memory of the elephant, he

did not remember decorating its forehead and trunk for the festive occasions. What happened to it anyway? he asked.

Since it had no religion, it was allowed to stay, his father said bitterly. I suspect it died of old age.

It was not as if we were not allowed to stay, said Debendranath Roy. We chose not to stay.

It depends on what you mean by choice, retorted his father.

It was easy for us, said his brother, but think of the poor peasants.

Once in a time of flood the villagers had gathered in the great gazebo that stood by their ponds, for their feudal home stood upon high ground, and was not readily inundated. The peasants had crawled in great crowds up the road to the grounds of their landlord's mansion, sheltered in the gazebo, been fed lentils and rice, while they watched for the rain to stop, waited for the waters to recede, and this he remembered, for Debendranath Roy had watched them from afar, intrigued by their manner, which later he came to recognize as resignation and patience, but which were quite incomprehensible to him then as human attitudes.

We were good to them, his father insisted, we were good to them. They were far better off before we were dispossessed.

Debendranath Roy remembered their faces, thick behind the curtain of rain, their eyes beating a slow time that was the pace of a different sort of life, one that he, at the age of four, had not yet identified as human.

You were good to them, he told his father, in the same way that a sensible farmer is good to his livestock.

I will not have this sort of impertinence from you, said his father. Do not think that I will tolerate this sort of impertinence from you just because I have allowed you to bring a white working class girl into my home.

Debendranath Roy put down the paper behind which he had been hiding when he made his remark. He stood up and brushed off the crumbs that Niharika had left upon his trousers while eating her bedtime biscuit upon his knee, as she had done every day, ever since she had suddenly sprouted the will to have a bedtime treat. He stood up, and brushed the crumbs from his trousers onto the Persian rug, left the room without a word to his father or brother, when they woke the following morning, he and his wife had gone, they would never see him again.

Azure

There was a biscuit tin in which her twin brothers kept their toy soldiers, it had a picture of an Englishwoman with a curlyhaired little girl, and this was how she imagined her aunt must look, for she had no memory of her face, and there were no photographs of her in any of the albums, although there were many of her uncle, her uncle who had drowned recently in faraway England. Sometimes, in the narrow room at the end of the corridor where they stored all the broken and useless furniture, she would crawl into an old rolltop bathtub that stood in the corner and pretend to drown among the dead leaves and moth carcasses. It was where she had her best adventures. She would spend hours there every afternoon while the others slept and her mother practised her music. Even when she only wanted to read, she preferred to sit against a heavy almirah tilted to the side on which it had lost a leg, and devour the book by the slatted sunlight of the tall shuttered window. It was there that she wrote her first story, about a prince who had been abducted by a magician who told the world that he was dead and kept him in a secret chamber, teeming with old furniture, in a castle in a land of dragons, far far away.

One day, one of the twins, in a fit of generosity, gave her the biscuit tin which she so covetted, and she tipped the soldiers out of it and took it away immediately to the junkroom and slipped it between the chickenclawed feet of the old bath, lest her brothers should want to reclaim it once they laid eyes upon it again. She kept her drawings and stories in it, carefully trimming the paper so that it would fit in nicely, and often she would take it out of its dusty niche just to stare at the face of the Englishwoman whom she imagined her aunt must look like, with her glossy brown hair parted straight down the middle of her head and gathered in two soft circles by her ears. She liked the row of buttons marching down the front of her dress, and the child in her arms, in all its white frills and golden curls, like the wax dolls that her mother kept locked in a glass cabinet in her drawing room, that she was only allowed to play with under strict supervision, which did not happen often because her mother was so busy always with her performances. She had started to act in plays as well as giving recitals, very serious plays that Niharika could not understand a word of. She fidgetted so much in the theatre that she was not allowed to go, but sometimes when the actors rehearsed in the house, she was allowed to watch. It fascinated her how they could switch in and out their roles so easily, all except her mother, who always seemed to take the part of herself. Years later she would wonder whether the plays were not written around the character of a woman like her mother, for the young playwright in their theatre group was clearly quite obsessed with her, treated her with a reverence that she found most comforting, even as a child. It was clear that her mother was quite different and she wondered if one day she too would command the same kind of respect, whether she too would cause the occupants of a room to draw their breath as she entered, as her silence filled its corners like stormlight, as her fragrance swept across their faces like the wrath of god.

Sometimes she would wonder if her mother actually had anyone, anyone at all, in mind when she sang with such passion of the pain of love, for that was the only time that the sky and the sea seemed not to meet in a clean line within her, but in a relentless scrambling of gullsong and brackenwind, when she sang with her eyes closed in the halfdark, *when did you place upon my neck this painful garland of love, I woke to see the clouds streaked red with the music of our parting, for you passed without waking me, clothed me while I slept in the sublime agony of your absence.* Niharika would stand quietly by the door, listening, until her mother saw her shadow, and asked if she would like to come and sing with her, or even learn a new song, if she was so inclined. Who did Tagore write these songs for? she was bold enough to ask once, hoping that in the answer there would be some clue as to whom it was that her mother seemed to address when she sang with such feeling. And her mother had replied that it was better sometimes not to address such things to any particular person, for people, she told her, come and go, but emotions last forever, and it is to celebrate the beauty of love rather than their lover that poets weave words together and steep them in song. This pleased Niharika, and she would sometimes wake with a great tenderness in her, that she felt ought to be the sweet sensation of being in love, although she could not attach it to anyone, no matter how hard she tried. After this conversation, she found it easier to exploit such a mood in writing her little stories, to make her damsels jump from tall towers upon hearing of the death of their beloved prince, it even struck her, as she sat with her head against the mossy pout of the old bathtub, wrapped in these mysteries, that her uncle might have drowned himself because of love. She saw him in the candleglow of an old cathedral, saying farewell to a tall, cruel woman, and walking down to the river afterwards to drown in the dark, but then she felt it was wrong to think of him like this, shook herself free of this bizarre fantasy, and went out to see if either of the twins would fancy a game of carrom.

Time passed, and her brothers grew into young men, one of them went off to an engineering college, the other stayed to go to a medical school in Calcutta. She had a series of crushes on their friends, but each dissolved in due course, especially if there were any signs that the interest might be mutual. She came to reconcile herself with the notion that it was only unrequited love that held any prolonged charm for her, that she preferred to adore from a distance, as she did some of her college professors, one or two of her mother's actor friends, all much older than her, and utterly unaware of the condition of her feelings. She had never had a relationship with a man when she came to Oxford at the age of twenty-three. She had even submitted, albeit reluctantly, to her father's search for an appropriate mate to accompany her, or better still already situated there, to guard and shelter her, but happily no such person was to be found. So she came alone to Oxford, followed her aunt's instructions to take the coach to Gloucester Green, where she would meet her. If I knew how to drive, I would come and pick you up at Heathrow, her aunt had written, of course I don't have a car, but if I knew how to drive I would have had a car, I should have learnt to drive, her aunt wrote, now it is probably too late. She found it hard to think of her now with the face of the Englishwoman on the biscuit box, darkened by grime, but still full of the stories she wrote when she was a child. At some point she had stopped writing, it was not clear exactly when, possibly after she had decided to embark upon a novel, they were on a seaside holiday, and she had spent her afternoons perched on a broad sill, biting her pencil, wondering what to do next with her characters, until the impossible breadth of it had overwhelmed her. She had met a vivacious young girl of her age on the beach, and spent the afternoons laughing with her instead. At the end of the two weeks, the girl went back with her parents to Delhi, they wrote to each other for long afterwards, but then lost touch. Strangely, as she prepared to go abroad to study, Niharika had been seized with the desire to renew her links with all those with whom they had lapsed, childhood friends who had moved away, friends made in other cities, friends made on holidays, she felt like gathering them to her like a basket of sparks, to tell them that they were still there somewhere within her, to assure them that although she was leaving the country, she was taking their memories, that they had planted something within her which would not stop to grow in a new climate, but perhaps be fostered with more care, like orchids in a hothouse.

Her aunt was waiting for her at the coach station, she looked too young to be forty, it was as if time had frozen upon her since the death of her husband, she looked small and helpless, standing there in her long raincoat, her long brown hair falling untidily over her eyes. They embraced, and Niharika had the absurd urge to say, don't worry, I will take care of you now, I am here now, it will be all right. Instead, she only held her tight, and let her spill a few tears into the dense wool of the old overcoat she wore, that she had dragged out of her grandmother's trunk, and insisted upon using, even though it was thirty-five years old, but it was intact and fit her perfectly, and it made her almost deliriously happy to think her grandmother had worn it once on a similar voyage, and that since then it had lain among the mothballs, waiting for resurrection in her hands. It still smelled of napthalene, despite much dry cleaning and airing, but that too had a certain holiness for her.

They took her suitcases to her college, were given the keys to her room, which was large but not bright. She looked out of the window at the quadrangle below filling slowly with scholars on their way to breakfast, and her aunt asked her whether she would like to sleep for a while, if she should go now and return later. She had slept on the plane, she said, and certainly was too excited to think of sleeping now. They had been asked to lunch, her aunt told her, by Professor Faraday and his wife, the professor had been an old mentor of her uncle's, it was he whom Debendranath Roy had come to see on the day of his drowning, they had both been very kind to her since she had moved to Oxford, and were keen to meet Debendranath Roy's niece, but would certainly understand if she was too tired to go. No, no, cried Niharika, she was not too tired, for the prospect seemed delightfully unreal, and so it was agreed that her aunt would go back and cook breakfast for her B&B guests, and then return around noon, and meanwhile Niharika would bathe and rest, and enjoy her first few hours in Oxford as she wished, before taking lunch with Professor Faraday and his wife in the village of Stanton St John. He picked them up at the porter's lodge at half past twelve, and she sat in the back of his small car in dreamlike contentment as they sped back along the route by which she

69

had entered the city a few hours ago. And then at the large roundabout which she recognized from her earlier encounter, they took a much narrower road, and within minutes drove up to the thatched cottage where he lived. They were not the only guests, for the Faraday's son Daniel was visiting from London. He had a little boy with him, but there was no sign of a mother, and for a while Niharika presumed that she was dead, until he mentioned his wife, and that she was away in Los Angeles on business, and it was strange to her, even though she had grown up with a mother who was so preoccupied with her profession, that a woman might leave a child in the care of her husband and go away on business. She saw him looking at her as she digested this fact. We are having a good time, said Daniel Faraday of himself and his son, as if he could read her mind.

Later, they took the boy for a walk, and as she stood watching the yellow of an autumn leaf so sharp against the darkness of the trees behind it, he said to her, it has always haunted me that I may have been the last person to see your uncle alive. I was driving him to the station, you see, he said, and as we crossed Magdalen bridge, he suddenly asked to be set down there, he said he had just remembered a few errands that he might as well run while he was there. Naturally, I obliged, and turning the car around, I saw him disappear in the direction of the river, which I thought was odd, but nothing more than just odd, until of course that evening the dreadful news came that he had been drowned.

They never found his body, she said.

He was doing the laces on one of his son's shoes, but he looked up quickly, and said without hesitation, do you think he might not have drowned.

It is one of my favourite fantasies, she admitted.

And mine, he said dreamily. I sometimes imagine that if I wait long enough beside the bridge, he will walk up the stone path again, and take up where he left off a dozen years ago.

She wondered what he did for a living that had not

consumed all his energy and imagination so he still had some left over to spill upon the memory of one of his father's students. Do you live in London? she asked.

We do, he said, and my wife would never want to move.

And you? she asked.

I travel a lot, he said, so it does not really matter, but sometimes I think it would be nice to come back to a house in the country, and I would rather he didn't grow up in London, he said gesturing towards his son who was playing with his grandfather's dog near the blackberry bushes.

And suddenly in this day of unreal people and unreal events, he seemed unbearably real to her, this man, her acquaintance of a few hours, the last person to have seen her uncle alive.

What do you do? she asked.

I take photographs, he said. Not art, he explained, I take photographs for people to use in advertisements. I like my job, he confessed.

A blackbird was looking at her boldly from its perch on a nearby bush, it reminded her of a mynah that she and her aunt had fostered in the year that she lived with them in Calcutta. There was nothing much wrong with it, but it had clearly been grateful for their attention, for it had come back regularly to share the squirrel's food, and had even amassed something of a vocabulary. After her aunt had gone, the bird would speak to her in her aunt's voice, or what she imagined was her aunt's voice, which always made her run into her room and cry.

And you? he asked. What will you be working on while you are here?

She told him that she had come to research the life of a pygmy who had been kept in the same cage as an orang utan in the Bronx Zoo in 1905, who had eventually been released but then had committed suicide in Virginia.

Something similar happened in a zoo in Switzerland, said Daniel Faraday. Clearly, to him, the project was not outside the bounds of the ordinarily absurd.

She felt a little annoyed that he had not reacted with more

surprise, as everyone else did, or at least with indignation, or even some embarrassment.

Instead he put his hands in his pockets and came and stood near her. I do not know whether I would mind, he said, I do not know whether I would mind being asked to share a cage with an ape.

How can you say so? she asked, completely taken aback.

He had fixed his strange blue eyes upon her, and laughed. I can imagine what they all say, he said, I can see them shaking their heads in disbelief, as if there is no fibre of their being that could have tolerated such a thing, as if they themselves would not, a hundred years ago, have brought their children to poke bananas through the bars for the sweet hominid, crouched in the corner upon his small bones.

That is no reason to be flippant about his condition, she objected.

What do you mean?

You said you would not mind being stuck in a cage with an ape.

Daniel Faraday shrugged. I can think of worse things, he said.

Like what? she challenged him.

Like being stuck in an office with a bunch of people you despise, doing something you despise, and then coming home to a wife you don't much like.

Would any one of these do? Or is it the whole combination that you think might be worse than being thrown in a cage with an ape for hundreds of people to gawp at all day?

He smiled. It would have to be a nice warm cage, he said, and I would need books, and good food and wine, but I would rather have an ape for company than most human beings.

What about all the people staring at you?

I think I could try and pretend they did not exist, he said.

I am sorry, he said, I do not mean to be rude or frivolous, it is just that I hate dishonesty of any sort.

Where does dishonesty come into it?

Only in the moral indignation that you expected me to affect when you mentioned it to me. I do think it is an interesting topic, and I wish you luck, and I hope I will see you again soon, said Daniel Faraday.

She did not see him again until the following spring, when he suddenly telephoned to say that he was coming to Oxford and wondered if he could take her out on the river as it was such a fine day. The year had passed quickly, and it was with a certain sadness that she had been sipping her tea and musing that so much had happened so quickly since she arrived, when the telephone rang, and it was him. They agreed to meet for lunch, and for a while afterwards she felt slightly resentful that within the space of a short telephone conversation he had managed to make all her rich and diverse experiences of these last months seem completely unworthy of being recounted, he had made her feel that nothing of value had really accrued within her life since she had met him, and when his car drew up outside the college gates, she realized that she was more nervous than she had been in a long time. And yet life had been so stocked with challenges recently that she had forgotten what it was like to feel truly incapable of a perfectly simple thing, to have lunch with a man she hardly knew, and feel that he was sure to want to have lunch with her again.

He stepped out of his car and came to her, kissed her upon both cheeks, which seemed a natural gesture, and opened the door for her. She realized, as he shut it after her, that some part of her had sorely missed, in these months, those elements of gentlemanly courtesy that her new male friends assiduously avoided, and which she herself had come to believe were part of the grand conspiracy to render all womankind as weak as wax dolls. And yet there was something so sensual in sitting back in the low seat of his rather creaky green sportscar, and feeling that he was in charge, as he guided the ailing vehicle through the maze of country roads to the pub where he wished to take her, she felt a delicious guilt creep over her, she wished that they might drive like this forever. She did not feel that she desired him, but that it was the situation that appealled deeply to her senses, the leather of the seat under her fingers, a woollen elbow peeping out of a hole in his waxed jacket, the vibrations of the car as it struggled from gear to gear.

I'm sorry about the car, he said, it is the first that I ever bought, I could not bear to sell it, and I keep it at my parents, drive it around when I am here, I came up by train last night you see, he explained.

This is the first car I have been in, she said, her eyes half closed, that feels like a car. All the rest seem to glide effortlessly about on your wonderful roads. I do not enjoy it.

I am glad to hear you say that, he said. A car should be hard work.

Everything should be hard work, she said.

Everything is, he replied.

And in his saying this, it abruptly became clear to her that she was, in her heart of hearts, deeply dissatisfied, and that the reason why she was so unfulfilled was that it had all been too easy since she had arrived, easy to dazzle with her beauty and her exotic wit, to impress with her erudition and creativity, to say the right things at the right time in just the right tone, it had all been too easy. And she saw that for her life to have meaning, she must set herself some other goal than to produce a stellar doctoral thesis. She envied Daniel Faraday that he could say nothing in his life came cheaply save the ease of driving a modern car.

She wondered as this old car coughed its way through the Cotswolds, whether it was the very one that he had used to transport her uncle, on a day much like this, thirteen years ago, when instead of taking him to the railway station, he had, at her uncle's request, dropped him off in front of the Botanical Gardens, turned the car around in Rose Lane, and watched with surprise as he saw Debendranath Roy disappear down the path to the river. What business could he have there? Daniel Faraday had wondered.

She tried to imagine what he might have been like then, a young man just out of college, uncertain of his future, and encumbered by the desire to make something extraordinary out of his life, and she was glad that it was her privilege to know him now, satisfied that his life was not extraordinary but would afford him the pleasure of shaping it largely as he wished. For the first time in her life she felt, of someone that she liked, that she was grateful not to have known him before. With him, she rejoiced in the great expanse of his life that lay outside her reach, his past and his present, his life then and his life now as a highly sought-after professional photographer, a dutiful husband and a loving father, a secure and mellow presence in the lives of the many, friends and family, who encircled him. And outside all of this, already, was she – this she sensed, as they drove in his old MGB through the sallow hills – that even though they hardly knew each other, her position in his life was unambiguously on the tangent that her uncle had created in Daniel Faraday's life, when instead of putting him on the train to London, he had let him drift down towards the river, thirteen years ago. I want to keep you as a mystery, he would tell her, a few years later, when it was clear to him that he loved her, on one hand I ache to know all of you, and yet I want to keep you as a mystery.

That is easy, she replied, for I am a mystery to myself.

It was New Year's Day, 1990, the begining of the last decade of the century. They were in a diner on Route 1 near Princeton, New Jersey, where she had come to work on her thesis for a year. She had grabbed the opportunity when it arose, it seemed obvious that she should leave Oxford for a while, for since that spring day when he had first come to visit her, they had seen each other often, and she had realized that she could not accept the torment of their fruitless passion with the same ease as he, and felt the best course for her was to go away. She had not seen him since the summer, and then on New Year's Eve he had telephoned, just as she prepared to spend it alone, in the house that she shared with five other graduate students who were all away. She had lit a fire, made herself a plate of scrambled eggs and bacon, and uncorked a bottle of wine to sip gently into the night, thinking how strange it was that she should be by herself on this evening which she and her friends in Calcutta had once planned to celebrate by trekking to Sandakfu in the Himalayan foothills, from there to see Everest by the first rays of the first dawn of the decade. And here she was instead in this cold creaky house alone, with only a housemate's pet snake to feed upstairs, when the telephone had rung, and it was he, Daniel Faraday, calling from Manhattan. I will come and see you tomorrow, if I may, he had said.

She was a little disappointed that he did not ask her if she was free to meet him in Manhattan, for it would have been a relief to jump on a train and spend the evening with him in Times Square or wherever he planned to be, to be dancing in his arms at midnight, or simply holding his hand as the clock struck twelve, and the eighties were irrevocably over. But perhaps he was worried that the easy magic of such a moment would enmadden them into actions that they would later regret. At any rate he did not ask her to join him then, but said that he would call for her in the morning, told her to make sure she did not drink too much or stay up too late, and this made her realize that he had taken for granted that, like everyone else in the world, she had other plans for the evening.

Goodnight my sweet, he said to her softly, and she felt her love for him expand in a vegetable fullness, like the growth of a tuber into the earth. She returned to the fire and the bottle of wine, and since the house was empty, she turned up the volume on the tape that she was playing of her mother singing some of her favourite songs, that she had put together in the few weeks that she had visited them last summer. It would be the last time that she would see them in her childhood home, for although they had no plans to sell the grand house, they had decided to move to Delhi and live in an adjoining apartment to the son who had made his home in that city. Her father had been diagnosed with a serious heart condition earlier that year, and this had prompted him to sell off the family business and retire. He had also suddenly become alarmingly religious, and she found that the old storeroom where she used to play had been cleaned out and transformed into a shrine, and a young woman who acted as a sort of secretary and nurse to him was expected to tend to the many idols, bathing and anointing them with sandalwood paste, offering them macaroons and fresh water in small bell metal tumblers every day, and putting them to bed before she left in the evening to make the long journey back to the refugee colony in the south of the city where she lived with her relatives. Her mother was indifferent to these proceedings, but produced for Niharika at one point the old biscuit tin still stuffed with her stories and pictures, and other oddments like a set of signatures of the English cricket team when the MCC came to play in India in the winter of 1976, which she had received as a token of a charity walk she had done at the time. I saved this from the garbage heap, Reba told her, when they were cleaning out the storeroom.

Her mother stood watching her as she sifted through the contents of the old tin box. Do you have time for such things at all these days, she asked, or is all of it taken up with research?

Niharika thought she sounded a little scornful, as if she felt that her daughter had made a strange choice channeling her creativity into academia rather than art and literature. You were a gifted storyteller, she said.

She did not recall telling stories to her mother, but it was true that her brothers and cousins had often listened for hours to her fantastic tales. A favourite game among them was 'Rigmarole' where someone started a story and others carried it forward in sequence, but she was always left till last to hold them spellbound as she gathered together all its threads, so much in danger of running away from each other, and knotted them into a spectacular denouement. Perhaps her mother, passing by, had stopped for a moment to listen, unbeknownest to her. I do not remember giving you any of these to read, she said, you would never have had the time to read them.

I know I neglected you, sighed Reba, but I did take an interest in your aesthetic development, if you had given me the stories I would surely have read them.

She smiled and asked, in what way did you take an interest in my aesthetic development?

I tried to teach you music, said her mother. Hours when I should have been rehearsing, I sat with you and tried to coax you to sing with me, I arranged for music lessons with the best masters, but you did not respond.

How can you say so, to learn a new song from you, to sit close to you and hear you sing, trace each phrase carefully for my benefit, and then wait for me to copy you, these are my best memories of childhood, said Niharika.

But you always seemed so distracted, said her mother.

Perhaps I was just mesmerized by you, she said. And then I was so desperately keen to please you, so desperately worried that you would give up on me and never ask to teach me to sing again.

When you have your own children, said Reba, you will know how wrong you were to think so.

I shall never have my own children, she said sadly.

And her mother instead of asking why she said so, came and sat down beside her, and stroked her head as it lay on the curve of the bedboard. You cannot always marry the man you love, she said, or indeed love the man you marry, but do not squander the gift of bearing children, for there is no other like it.

She did not find herself soothed by her mother's words or even by her gentle hands upon her head.

When you were a baby, I used to sit and watch you, said Reba, I used to sit and watch you sleep and I could not believe that anything so beautiful could be alive. For some reason I was left alone with you more than I was with the boys — perhaps because there were two of them, and certainly because

I was a novice. Besides, they were an event in the family's history, you were simply mine.

Niharika turned her head towards her, so that the teak edges of the bedboard cut into her cheek, will you do something for me, she asked, if I write down a list of my favourite Tagore songs, will you tape them for me in your voice?

With the greatest pleasure, promised her mother.

You see no one sings them as you do, said Niharika.

And now, in the firelight, she listened over and over again to the tape that Reba had made for her. Outside the wind howled, and the snow blew in fine white clouds like unclothed banshees prowling the narrow empty streets, she wrapped herself in bright blankets, held her toes as close as she dared to the fire, and listened to her mother's voice, singing: *if the doors to my heart should close upon you someday, I beseech you to break them down and not turn away defeated*, and sobbed with relief that she was to see him again, for when she had told him six months ago that she was going to spend the following academic year in Princeton, he had agreed, without much obvious anguish, that it would be the best thing for her and for them if she went away for a while.

I needed to know, he told her the following morning, how long I could survive without you.

And? she asked, looking up from her blueberry pancakes, life was a string of endless breakfasts for her in this country, she thought.

And now I know, he said, removing the huge bottle of maple syrup that stood between them and placing it carefully on the narrow window sill.

What do you know? she asked.

I know that I could live without you forever, live within the holy order of my life in London, and savour my few memories of you for the rest of my life.

Then why are you here now? she asked, humbled by his confession.

Because I cannot imagine that you feel the same, he said.

So you are here because you think I cannot possibly live without you? she said.

That is not the only reason.

He let his fingers rest upon hers, and she knew then that this asymmetry of wanting had no particular significance for their relationship, it only meant that she would spend her days sitting by the fire, drinking wine and longing to be with him, while he would ease his way through his many professional and social engagements, his family duties, thinking of her, but reconciled to her absence.

I will try and be patient, she promised him.

I do not want to have taught you to be patient so early in life, he said, for it is a time when patience has no value, no at your age, you should be horribly impatient to make your mark upon the world, that is how I was, said Daniel Faraday, slightly wistfully.

And now that you have made your mark upon it, you can afford to be patient? she asked.

Patience is a luxury, he said, that one should not cultivate too early. Sometimes I worry that I have too much of it, but it has made things easier for me and for the people I love.

It will not make it easier for me, she said.

No, it will not, he sighed. And this is what I have come to tell you, even though it breaks my heart. My wife and I have decided to move to Australia for a few years, and so when you come back to Oxford, I will no longer be in the country. I do not think we should agree not to see each other again, for I know that there will be times when I will be driven mad with the longing just to set eyes upon you, but let us think of our times together as a collection of precious gems, that we might add to sometimes, but only if the right moment arrives.

A collection of precious gems? she said. Surely you can do better than that?

Even I am allowed to be trite sometimes, he said. You must

grant me that. It is an appropriate analogy, if you feel strongly about gems.

You know I do not, she said.

Yes, I know you do not care much for jewels, but I hope you will let me give you this, he said, taking out of his pocket a box which he handed across to her. In it was a fine filigree brooch in the shape of sailboat, with a single small diamond on the top of its mast.

She held it gently between her fingers and smiled, *there were crumpets in the cabin, and apples in the hold*, she quoted slowly from a nursery rhyme whose words he had taught her. They had been driving to Tintern Abbey, not in his old MGB, but in the faceless stealthy new car that he used more regularly, she had found a tape of nursery rhymes that he kept in his glove compartment to entertain his son, and she had asked if she might listen to them. Of course, he said, and then had spent most of the journey interpreting them for her, for most of the rhymes were sung or recited in heavily regional accents. I don't really know what a crumpet looks like, she had confessed, although I remember using it in a story that I wrote as a child, a story about English children who come home after an adventure to crumpets for tea. It was the only story that she had written in English, as a sort of challenge, she had torn it up immediately afterwards.

The sails were made of silk, and the masts were all of gold, he finished for her. She remembered her first sight of the Abbey, the drama of its sudden appearance against the mellow slopes of the Wye Valley, it had filled her with a great and amorphous hope. They had sat for hours in its eastern shadow, simply talking, and it had become clear to her then that her pleasure in his company was not simply that of a young woman relishing the attentions of a more mature and deeply fascinating man, that it was not just the tenuous mystery of her uncle's disappearance that connected them, but something much more subtle. He affected her in a way that she could not define, she thought of him almost constantly in the days that followed, and it filled her with a profoundly rich ease, a self-enclosed sweetness that made her shun the company of her eager new-found friends, and spend much time clositered in her room with her books. She would have been content, then, not to have seen him again, to have let the music of that afternoon spent in the shade of the grand ruins of Tintern Abbey run along the riverbed of her thoughts for a long time, until eventually it would sink leaving a fine trace of gold dust where it had run for so long.

One morning, soon after, she found in her mailbox a parcel from him containing a new copy of the nursery rhymes tape. Playing it in the gloom of her woodpanelled room, she had found that the joy she felt was edged with an uncompromising blue, she turned it off and put it away, she would only play it later when she knew that she had the strength for the pain and happiness that it brought.

The four and twenty sailors that stood between the decks were four and twenty white mice with chains about their necks, his son would repeat to her one afternoon a few months later, when she and her aunt were at tea with Professor Faraday and his wife, and Niharika had been left to entertain him while the others played Scrabble. His parents were at a wedding in Hampshire. She had spent the entire time terrified that they would turn up while she and her aunt were still there and soon after the tea things were cleared away she pleaded with her aunt to return to Oxford. I have a lot of work to do, she tried to explain. But I want to go for a walk, the boy protested, and seeing his grandparents and her aunt setting up a game of Scrabble, she realized that there was nothing for it but to take him for a long walk, and hope that Daniel would have the sense to delay their journey, although she was not entirely convinced that he had not deliberately engineered the situation, or at least had allowed it to happen, relishing its easy irony. Trooping through the fields, they came upon a hedge-hog, and the many questions that he asked about its habits, and the fantastic responses that she made up for him, quickly led to a long and marvellous tale, like those she would make-up for her brothers and cousins when they were children. Emboldened by its telling, she returned to the cottage, ready to meet, if she must, the wife of the man she loved, but although he was there, she was not. She had an appointment in London to keep, and finding the boy gone, they had agreed that she would drive straight on, and he and the boy would take the train later, or even the following day.

Will you have dinner with me tonight? he asked her in front of the assembled company.

I have a lot of work to do, she said, astonished by his open familiarity.

That can wait, surely, he said. I've booked a table at Studley Priory – it's just down the road – even the MG will be able to crawl that far.

She thought how strange it would be in Calcutta for him to ask her to dine with him without inviting his parents and her aunt. In their house, if anyone announced that they were planning to eat at a restaurant it would be assumed that anyone who wished to might accompany them, even the children, as long they were willing to stay up and had finished homework. So often she had wished to be alone with her parents and her brothers, but some visiting relatives or friends would invariably tag along. She looked around, almost helplessly, at her aunt and Professor and Mrs Faraday, but they only smiled and encouraged her to enjoy the evening, and leave her studies till the morrow.

Put her in a taxi though, said her aunt. I don't want you driving her back after a boozy dinner, especially in that car of yours.

It is not as if they do not know that I see you sometimes, Daniel said to her later as they were sipping their aperitifs. Besides we have never done anything that we need to conceal from anyone.

I was terrified that I would have to meet your wife, she said.

83

I did not know you were there, he said. But I think you would like her. I do, he said.

I am sure I would like her, but that does not mean it would be easy to meet her, she replied.

Come and walk with me, he said, laying his arm lightly across her shoulders, let us walk outside.

It is misty and cold, she said.

I know, but it will be nice.

And as they walked upon the grass, clutching their cold glasses, he tightened his hold upon her and said, I came out to see if I could find you, after Alison had gone, I went out to see if I could find the two of you, but when I spotted you I felt I did not want to go any further, I stood and watched you, you were irresistible in the mist, he said.

Her foot hit a croquet hoop, she stooped and picked up a mallet that lay beside it – what is this? she asked.

Have you never seen them playing in college? he asked her.

I have seen the hoops and the balls, but never found out how they were used.

Let me demonstrate, he said, looking around for the balls.

But there were no balls to be found, and he had to knock imaginary ones through the mist to show her how the game was played, it was all so cheerfully surreal that the danger was suddenly averted of the evening being engulfed by the tragedy of their love. Dinner was heavenly, and the wines agreed with her untutored palate, even though she could not appreciate them in the way that he did, he always enjoyed what she had to say of an unfamiliar taste, that truffles had the same flavour as a delectable Bengali riverfish, that a cocktail she did not like reminded her of camel urine, which she had never tasted of course.

I have missed you, he told on New Year's Day, 1990, in the overheated diner on Route 1, where they had had to drive to find any sort of food. They had walked up and down Nassau Street, dazed to be in each other's company again, in such a harsh cold, until he had cursed and said that their only hope of finding anything open was to drive out of town. He was planning to drive down later to Washington DC to see some friends, his wife and child would join him there later in a day or two, and then they were to escape to some more temperate clime. Although in this cold, he said, it seems hard to believe that there is anywhere on this planet that's warm and sunny, it's hard to see beyond the horizons of this frozenness, he complained.

I have missed you, he said, and I will miss you. I suspect that every day I will see something or do something that I will desperately want to tell you, certainly that is how it has been in these last months.

We never did go punting, she said, fingering the boat brooch.

For indeed, on that first spring day that he had come to see her, the sky had darkened quite suddenly as they ate, and before lunch was over, the rain had come lashing down, and so instead they had gone to the Ashmolean, where he had shown her some of the things he particularly liked, and in the room of musical instruments, she had suddenly, for the first time since she had arrived in Oxford, specifically longed for her mother. She had been homesick of course, but in a very general way, which the excitement of being in a foreign land had made quite manageable, but here in this room of viols and mandolines, the desire to see her mother gripped her like a nausea, and this she found ominous. Later in the spring and summer, she would go out on the river with her friends, but never with him, for it never felt like the right thing to do again to glide together serenely down the river when all else between them was so unquiet, so much in tumult.

We never did go punting, she said, thinking that if they were in a boat now, she would surely have driven the stake through its bottom.

Someday we will, he promised, not very soon, but someday, we will.

I'd like to go back now, she said, feeling that she might cry soon.

Of course, my love, he replied. I want to ask you something. I have a friend in Manhattan who has just come out of an asylum, he is an extraordinary man, I'd be grateful if you would visit him sometimes, he had said.

You want me to visit a mad friend of yours in New York?

He is not mad, said Daniel, he is just manic depressive, and that too you would never know from just being with him. In fact, he radiates the sort of calm that instils a calmness in you. I learnt a lot from him in the year that I spent in New York, when I was just a frenzied youth, and he seemed to have a window on a part of life that I had never even caught a glimpse of before.

But why would he want to meet me? she asked.

I think you would cheer him up like nobody could, he said.

He wrote down the name and telephone number on a napkin, folded it and gave it to her, and when later she opened it she found the single name – Morgan – whether it was his first or last she had not been told, nor ever would know.

How is the pygmy? he asked as they drove back through the snow.

Alive and kicking, she replied dully.

Did you know, he asked, that there was once a scheme – in the early nineteenth century I believe – to populate the New England forests with all of the creatures in Shakespeare's plays?

Not Puck and Titania or Caliban, I presume?

No, just the real ones, he said.

And did it succeed? she asked.

I believe it is how the starling came to be such a ubiquitous bird in these parts, said Daniel Faraday.

He pulled up outside the house, and she turned to say goodbye to him, but the words froze upon her lips, and he, reaching to stroke her cheek, let his hand fall upon her shoulder, and simply looked into her eyes. They sat, with the engine purring grimly, and the windscreen filling with snow, looking at each other, until he took the key out of the ignition and asked her quietly if he might come in. Once they were inside, he took her in his arms, and covered her face with kisses. You do understand what you mean to me, don't you? he asked, you won't doubt how I feel about you simply because I can live with the idea of not seeing you again?

No, no, she assured him, breaking gently free of his hold. She began to clear away the plate and knife and fork and wineglass from her meal of the previous evening, when she had sat by the fire nursing the precious hope that somehow a solution would materialize to their situation. Well here was a solution, she thought, the most trivial of all solutions, to simply part, possibly forever.

He followed her into the kitchen. How many of you live here? he asked.

There are six of us, she said, the others are away.

He stood behind her, stroking her hair, as she washed the few things in the sink, it is the first time we are in a house together by ourselves, he said, it feels strange.

It is also the last time, she reminded him.

Can we not forget that for a moment? he asked. It is so good to be with you like this, he said, it is perhaps what I have most wanted always, to be with you in an empty house, perfectly sealed from the world outside, to bring you a warm mug of tea when you wake up, to hear you in the shower, or playing on the piano in a room at the other end of the house.

In my dream, he continued, the house is a little underheated, it is not a house we regularly inhabit, warmly congested with the toing and froing of our everyday lives, it is the sort of house where we wear heavy woollen jumpers, and find that the taps in the basement which worked last year don't work anymore, so that I cannot use it as a darkroom, and this makes me a little grumpy, but you dig out a telephone book from one of the kitchen closets, and we manage to find a plumber, but he is not keen to drive out so far so late, so instead we go for a walk in the snow, the trees dripping lozenge icicles, in my dream, he said, moving away from her slightly, as if he feared that the images might uncluster if he were too close to the object of his desire.

In my dream, he said, your hair is always slightly damp, and never so long, and I can run my hands through it while I kiss you.

And then for the first time he kissed her upon her lips, kissed her and kissed her, until their movements together took on its own logic, as easily as salt flowing into sand, he unbuttoned her warm tunic and began to stroke her breasts, my sweet, my sweet, he said, kissing the curve of her shoulder, and then he lifted her into his arms and carried her back to the living room, put her down gently on the rug, and there they made love, as she had imagined fearfully they might, the night before, when she sat there alone and thought of him, and felt that if he were to try to make love to her, she would not wish to be able to resist. Afterwards they lay in delicious embrace for a long time upon the motheaten rug, watching the snow fall thicker and faster through the window at the far end of the room, I could phone my friends and say I got stuck in the storm, he said, I could stay until tomorrow.

His voice sounded to her as if it came through stone, as if she were in a deep well with an ear pressed to the wall, I do not think you should stay, she said. It seemed impossible to her that they might to do something ordinary now, like try and find some lunch, end up in the same diner where they had eaten breakfast, or even drive to New York in search of some human life, it seemed that none of these things could happen now.

You are right, he said, I should go.

Perhaps I will never see you again, he said. He kissed her upon the cheek and walked towards the door.

Before he left, he said, if you have to forget me, do it in a way that I will be able to bear.

What way is that? she asked.

Suspend me in something soft, he said, don't let me wither and lose my colour in some acrid liquid, or embalm and wrap me into a shapeless bundle.

That will never happen, she promised.

He looked back one last time. And you will visit that friend of mine in New York, won't you? he said.

I will, she replied.

JADE

A week after she parted with Daniel Faraday, she took the train to New York to meet his friend Morgan. He was waiting for her at Penn Station, smoking a pipe, tall and rather asthenic in appearance, but more neatly and conventionally dressed than she had imagined. I don't like to meet new people, he told her, but Faraday said you would be worth it.

Did he? she said.

Do you like Japanese food? he asked. I find I can't eat anything but sushi these days, when I eat anything at all.

I have never had sushi, she told him, although I do know what it is.

The English are not big on Japanese cuisine, are they?

There are no Japanese restaurants in Oxford, she said, but I know there are many in London, but they are very expensive apparently.

Sushi is not the cheapest of foods, said Morgan, but my parents left me a shitload of money, so much money I don't know what to do with it, especially as I myself like to do nothing, and plan to do nothing for the rest of my life.

And how would you have done that, she asked, if your parents hadn't left you so much money.

Oh, I'd have found a way, he said.

They took a cab through the city to the restaurant he had selected. Confronted by the massive vertical grandeur of Manhattan, she felt a deep release, as if she had finally reached the shores of an ocean, and was finally able to breathe. *Where is the open wind of the endless sea to soothe all my sores? When will I hear the regal thunder of the ocean? For I sit dreaming upon the shores of this river, while the best of times passes me by*, so the poet had written, and nothing now better captured her state of being. Here was the ocean then, where she might fall upwards and breathe deeply of its encrusted dark, I must come here more often, she thought.

They arrived at their destination, a Japanese restaurant as Morgan had promised, whose walls were painted a chilly luminous grey, the tables and chairs were black and sunken into the floor which flowed seamless into the walls. She was amused by the decor, but wished there were more warmth in the eccentricity.

You do not like the decor, observed Morgan.

It's a bit like a bad skin condition, she said.

He laughed. Faraday was right, you do have a curious imagination.

He loves you, you know, he said later.

Her cheeks grew warm, she said nothing.

He's not the kind of guy who leaves his wife, though.

Have you met her? she asked, realizing suddenly that he was her first confidant, for somehow she felt that she had already entrusted him with her feelings, or that Daniel Faraday had done so for her, what is his wife like? she asked.

Oh, she's great, he said, flicking shavings of pink ginger across his plate. She's hideously capable, which is just what Faraday needs.

Why do you think so? she asked, for she had always felt that he had a great urge to protect and nurture, and never that he needed much support himself.

Faraday needs to dream, said his friend.

So?

She gives him the freedom to dream, said Morgan, whereas you would not, you see you are all he could ever want.

You are making this up as you go along, aren't you? she said.

Somewhat, he admitted.

She laughed, and took a long sip of the excruciatingly cold rice wine.

You are in a lot of pain, he observed.

94

How do you know? she asked.

Because I am in love with him myself, said Morgan, but he will never love me, or even think of loving me as he loves you.

I see, she said, surprised that she was not more amazed by this unexpected confession.

You think you are better off than I am, don't you, he said in a moment or two. You think that at least he loves you.

But you will probably see him again, whereas I will not.

That cannot be, said Morgan. I am sure that he will come back to see you.

And briefly she was lit by a thin sliver of presentiment that he would come back or at least telephone her soon. But then she was plunged again into the eerie grey opalescence of the Japanese restaurant. Would you like any coffee? Morgan asked.

No, she said, it keeps me awake.

Which you do not need, he agreed.

You will come again, won't you? he asked as he called for the bill.

Why don't you come down to Princeton? she asked.

Because I promised myself at graduation never to go back.

You went to Princeton?

Years and years ago, said Morgan.

Was it hell? she asked.

No, actually it was wonderful, he said, it was stiflingly wonderful.

And now, he said, I'm going to send you home by cab.

All the way to Princeton?

That's where home is, isn't it?

But I can take the train, she protested.

I am going to get a cab to take you home, because you have been excellent company, because I want to send you home that way, and because I can.

In the months that remained of her time in the country, she saw him very regularly, for he would send a car down to fetch

95

her once or twice a week, and they would spend the afternoon wandering around the city, eat dinner somewhere, go back to his flat and talk late into the night. He decided he could not subject her constantly to sushi, so they would try and find a restaurant where she could eat a proper meal and he could pick one item that was palatable to him, usually oysters, which he would consume at incredibly long intervals in order to give her the time to eat her lamb steaks or monkfish tails. He was like a gift that Daniel had given her in apology for his absence, a colourful and intelligent companion, an expensive kaleidoscope that a father might leave on his child's pillow before he embarks upon a long journey. And, unlike Daniel, he found the pygmy in the Bronx Zoo deeply fascinating. He insisted that they go there to see exactly where the atrocity took place, he was amazed that she had not been there already, you academics, you fucking kill me, he said. He spent hours in the library hunting out newspaper articles that might have mentioned the pygmy, he found the addresses of nonagerians who might remember the event, or even have been to see the creature. It was as if her project had given him a new lease on life. Before she left, he arranged a trip for them to Virginia to visit the house where the pigmy had finally lived as a human, and where he had eventually taken his own life. It was because of him that she ceased to think of the pygmy purely as part of the analytical exercise of obtaining a D. Phil, and instead as a character in the peculiar drama she had set out to investigate, and in which she had enlisted Morgan. And once he became a living breathing thing, her imagination – which had made so much out of far less – seized him and wove him into an endless string of fantasies, which she felt compelled to write down, first in Bengali, but later in English, and when this happened, she showed what she had written to Morgan.

This is amazing, he told her, I have never read anything like this.

His encouragement was so precious to her that when the book was finished, many months later, she felt she should dedicate it to him, in some oblique way it would also be a dedication to Daniel, which was what she really wished, but finally she dedicated it to her mother. Morgan had introduced her to a literary agent in New York, who managed to sell it for her within a year to a very prestigious publishing house, and soon after the British rights were purchased by a house of equivalent standing in London. The shock of it numbed her to everything, including Daniel's absence, for a long time. Terrified that she was starting to forget him, she shut herself away and devoted herself to finishing her thesis, relishing the task of recasting the same material in an utterly different mould. The two would mirror and mock each other, she thought. And then by degrees her mind began to fill sweetly again with thoughts of him, she imagined how he might stumble upon her face in a bookshop, buy the book and read it, recognize the character that was Morgan and feel horribly jealous, for nowhere within the pages, unless he looked harder within them than she had, would he find any trace of himself. Then she panicked that he would think that she had forgotten him, that he would muse that it was just as well that he had ceased to occupy such a large part of her life, for she herself had perhaps shrunk within him to a mere delicate memory, she had had no indication in the two years since she had last seen him that it was any other way.

But now she had the courage to accept this, she realized. Now that the world had already offered her so much, the exhilaration of writing the book, the peculiar reality that it would be in the bookshops in a few months, the time spent with Morgan chasing the story of the pygmy's existence, the comradeship that had cemented like a set of misshapen rocks between them, that she had come to value so greatly. He had not visited her since she had returned to Oxford for he loathed air travel, but they had written long letters to each other, and had spoken to each other over the telephone almost every week. On the day that the news came that the book had been accepted by a New York publisher, a hamper arrived from

Harrods in his name, loaded with champagne and sushi, and other more endurable delectables. Later he telephoned, have they all gone? he asked.

Who? she said.

Well, you didn't eat all that sushi on your own, did you?

No, that I did not.

But now they are gone, and you are lonely, even though you did not want them there in the first place.

You read me like a book, Morgan.

Better than a book, he said.

It was true, he always seemed to know what she was thinking, always found a way to make her confess. She remembered how when they were driving down to Virginia on the trail of the pygmy, he had suddenly said to her:

Celibacy is quite a reasonable option for a man of my inclinations, especially with the dread virus at large. But for you, my dear, to save yourself for a man you will never have, is patently ridiculous.

She had said nothing, looked out onto the sea of cars slowly sailing past them on the motorway.

He has slept with you, then, said Morgan bitterly.

Only once, she had longed to say, only once, only the last time, so that the guilt of it would be diminished by the resolution never to see me again.

What an irresponsible bastard! said Morgan.

The responsibility is as much mine as his, she found herself protesting, and then despite herself, she began to tell him how it had happened, to absolve her lover of the sin of having ravished her without caution, of having taken advantage of her helplessness.

The last thing he did before he left was to remind me of my promise to visit you, she told Morgan as they sped southwards in the back of the car that he had hired to take them to the scene of the pygmy's freedom and demise.

I bet he was feeling terrible, said Morgan, chewing on his sunglasses.

Have you heard from him at all? she asked tremulously.

Christ, no, said Morgan, we would never write to each other.

How does he know where to find you then?

I have never moved from that apartment, not since I first rented it twenty years ago, and I don't intend to move ever, and if I do I will certainly take my phone number with me.

Can you do that?

He looked at her, there's so much you don't know about how things work here, he said, it's quite delightful, I could spend hours just amusing you with silly little facts, which is I suppose why certain people like to associate with foreigners.

They are like jellybeans though, these novelties, too many of them and your mouth feels tired and stale.

But it's the thrill of something like a new system of mixer taps that keeps all these people alive and contented, keeps their hearts beating, last night I saw an advertisement for a correct posture dog feeder, can you imagine? he said.

I did see some tins of low calorie dog food in the supermarket the other day, she said.

No, those are useful, he said, if you have a hypertensive dog.

She started to laugh, I'm sure they are indispensable in that sort of situation, she said.

I am not joking, said Morgan.

Sometimes she thought of trying to live in New York, as a writer or an academic, for she knew that even when she was down to her last resources, she could not fail to be amused by Morgan, that in him she had found a companion like no other. She was confident that their obscure and purely Platonic friendship could sustain her forever, this friendship devoid of any physical yearning, not even the simple need to hold and touch that she had felt with all her female friends, her cousins and brothers. Oh she could live forever with Morgan, in his unruly Upper West Side apartment, and Daniel could come and visit them sometimes, although it was not that they were united only in their love for him, though he was sure to think so. It was much more than that, so much more than that, Morgan had opened up a whole new region of riddles within her, from which sprouted other riddles, it was with him that she had first truly come to rejoice in her own sense of humour, for although she knew that Daniel delighted in her quirky imagination, she felt almost always like a clever child when she said something that amused him. With Morgan she felt that she was entirely in control of her words and actions, it was as if they were engaged in continuously solving a most marvellous puzzle, of which the conundrum of the pygmy formed only a small but absorbing part.

He nourished her desire to amuse, to amuse an equal as an equal. So much of her life she had felt she was performing for the benefit of those who were older and wiser, and lately more that she was entertaining individuals who had not the capacity to appreciate her, bright and capable as they were within their own spheres, her fellow students, her friends, her cousins and brothers. With Morgan she had laughed as she had never laughed before in her life, or since. She had found it easy to throw back her head and simply roar with laughter. Before, she had never been comfortable with any excess of expression. She would sit uncomfortably still in a crowd of children when they were watching cricket together, and someone scored a crucial boundary or took an important wicket, around her they would scream in childish glee, and she would smile and bounce a little, hoping that her lack of obvious enthusiasm passed unnoticed. I have never laughed like this, she told Morgan, wiping her eyes after he had read to her from a scrapbook that he collected of unusual news items. Perhaps it's because you are a virgin no longer, he said. Morgan, you are cruel, she said, but it did not seem to hurt her that he constantly referred so flippantly to such a precious moment in her life, wheedled her for details that she refuse to provide, was he any good then? he would ask, was he good in bed, Faraday? How would I know? she would answer, I have nothing to compare it with. Well, perhaps you should then? he would say. Should what? she would ask. Should go and find somebody to compare him with, he would answer. What, find someone to sleep with, solely for the purpose of being able to tell you where he ranks as a lover? she would say. Why not? he would persevere. Dream on, Morgan.

She felt it would be worth moving to New York to be with him again, to find ease for her soul in his unremitting wit, to drench her faculties with their shared sense of the absurd, to cultivate irony as an escape from love. Perhaps as they grew older they would finally emerge from Daniel Faraday's clutches, and roam the city like two tired vampires in search of an inexperienced youth that they might both adore in their separate ways, who would be drawn into their lair for nights of long conversation and wild make-believe, and emerge afterwards a little less sure of himself and his inclinations, but vastly better for it. Once, in a furniture shop, he had pretended that they were engaged to be married. He had dragged her there to buy a new mirror after his antique looking glass had swivelled a fraction too far and ended up in fragments on the polished parquet, he had pretended to the overattentive shop assistant that they had come to decide on their wedding list, and it had amazed her how easily she had slid into this bizarre game, judging each piece as it might inhabit an imaginary house. What enormous pleasure there was to be gained in this deception, in the simple mimicry of a whole class of people that she hardly knew. Morgan of course had had to spend his whole life among them, so his enjoyment was tinged with the glory of revenge, while part of hers was wistful, she imagined that Daniel would have gone through all of this in earnest in the same sort of shop in London before his wedding. She saw him poring over an album of cutlery patterns with his wife, and could not find it in herself to feel any contempt.

Perhaps he would marry her, Morgan, just for the farce of it. They would have a splendid Hindu wedding in Calcutta, everyone would be happy that she had found such a charming, rich and cultured American, and they would spend the rest of their lives in cheerful unconsummated cohabitation, with long periods away from each other of course lest the irony of the situation should become too overpowering.

They could even adopt a child, she mused. Nothing in her life so far had been more rewarding than the company of children. Recently when her parents had come to visit her in Oxford, they had brought with them her niece. It had been arranged that they would stay with Jennifer, and that Niharika would spend time with them whenever she could. She had warned her parents that it was not a good time to visit her, as she had set herself a deadline for her thesis, but they had ignored this, for they planned to travel on to Dallas, Texas afterwards to be with their other son and his wife in the last stages of her confinement and then help take care of the baby. Niharika was annoyed that they had been so little concerned with her incovenience and had resolved not to make any particular effort for them, but her niece had captivated her instantly, and it was to see her that she would tear herself away from her work and walk down the network of traffic-ridden roads to her aunt's B&B near the railway station.

One afternoon, shortly after they had arrived, she came across them on her way to the B&B, Reba and the child, sitting together under Hythe Bridge, and she felt almost as if she were trespassing upon a private garden, as she watched her mother gaze with the grace of a monarch's wife upon the sluggish waters. She stood watching them, with a strange, somewhat heady, sensation of guilt, as they sat in this strange oasis, the traffic screaming around them upon Hythe Bridge and Park End, they sat, her mother with her granddaughter, the child's hand in hers, insulated by her dignity. Her majestic radiance appeared to transform even this most public of situations into a secluded corner of some royal garden, and yet never before was it clearer to her how small were the kingdoms over which her mother had been granted dominion, a petty patch of waterside in this foreign land, the limited society of her peers in Calcutta, the narrow halls of her husband's home.

You have written a book, have you not? her niece asked her, can I read it?

You can, she said, but it is full of big words that you might not know yet.

And that evening the girl proudly showed a page that she had copied from a dictionary that she had somehow located in these largely bookless premises. Can I have it? Niharika had asked, and she had kept it since then among her most precious things.

How she would like to have a little daughter to hold in her arms while they slept, to help draw pictures of dragons and rabbits, to balance upon her knee and tell tales of magic caskets and men who disappeared into underwater kingdoms, married mermaids and were never seen again. Was it all really never to be? Since she had returned from the United States, she had met a few men who excited her imagination in a moderate way, she felt she might learn to like them if she tried, if it meant that she might settle down somewhere and have children, but then it would become clearer to her than ever that it was not just children she wanted but a life that she could call her own, with its own tender boundary between herself and everything else that might happen to her, membranes that would swell and rust and heal again to enclose her in the noble purpose of living, of tending a fire, or making ravioli, or tapping hardboiled eggs upon a marble slab, was it all never to be?

Her niece went back a week earlier than her parents, and was entrusted to the care of a charming stewardess on a direct flight to Delhi. Niharika took her down to the airport on the coach.

Will you come and see me? the girl asked.

Very soon, she replied.

Will you write to me?

Every week.

She watched her disappear, her thin shoulders clenched against the arm of the pretty stewardess, and was overwhelmed by a strange sense of guilt, as if she was bound to let the child down someday, even though she had done nothing to dismay her yet. Meanwhile she would write to her every week, as she had promised.

The year that followed was filled with travelling to conferences and literary festivals, to present her pygmy in his many different guises – as her research material, her muse, her friend, philosopher and foe – and from each new place she would religiously send her niece a postcard. She had thought that she would not have much to say to her, but invariably her writing would begin to spill into the address box and wind its way around the already affixed stamp, and the girl wrote back lovely long letters, carefully written in curly joined hand. They were the first things she would look for in her college mailbox when she returned from a trip, and still she would dream recurrently in vivid detail that the child was famished in a railway carriage while watching a family tuck into their picnic and trying to swallow back her own hunger, and from this dream she would wake and sob hard into her pillow, until the ache of this would merge into the grander pain that never left her, of Daniel's absence, and her sobbing would become an outlet for both.

She had not heard from him once since they had parted, although she was kept informed of their movements by his mother, whom she saw quite regularly. She would often come into town without Professor Faraday, and ask her to lunch with her at the Old Parsonage, where the two of them would sit for hours in a corner and talk. There was in her a particular sense of satisfaction with life that Niharika had never found in either her mother or in Jennifer, a treacly gravity that was profoundly connected to the rituals of womanhood that engirdled her, and from which she would never think to escape, while her mother had tried so hard, it seemed to Niharika, to run away, to reinvent herself in her music, and somewhere had failed. As for Jennifer, poor sweet Jennifer, she sometimes wondered if life would have been any better for her if her uncle had not drowned in the Cherwell eighteen years ago, whether the yoke of widowhood suited her any less than the candyfloss of affection without respect, which was all he probably had to offer her when she was his wife. Rosemary Faraday spoke often of her son, she had no reason to believe after all that this might cause any pain. Rosemary Faraday told her of how he had been as a boy, her son Daniel, now approaching his fortieth year, and Niharika would wonder sometimes whether she would have liked her at all as a daughter-in-law, for it was clear she did not get on so well with his wife. Alison will wake up one day and realize that her life has passed her by, Rosemary Faraday said to her, she never has any time for her family, for a walk in the park, for a lunch like this, one day she will regret it, I know.

And then the time came for her to make the journey to New York that they had planned for so long, she and Morgan, an opportunity also of course to promote her book. He met her at the airport rather formally dressed, I thought we would go straight on to dinner, he explained, tugging at his bowtie.

Morgan had put on a bit of weight, she noticed, and he ate a three course meal with her for the first time since she had known him. My aversion to food seems to have disappeared since my grandmother died last year, he explained, perhaps she took the memories with her of all those ghastly mealtimes at the long dining table with them, eating in silence and wishing I could just stand up and piss in my soup. I thought tomorrow we might drive out to a wonderful Peruvian restaurant I found in the most unlikely town upstate, he said.

But I have a reading to do tomorrow, she said, and will probably have to go out with them afterwards. You are invited, of course.

His face darkened a little. You know how much I hate company, he said, but I will come if you want me to.

Later, she wished she had not asked him, for as soon as they had walked into the bookshop, he grabbed her arm and pulled her between two tall bookshelves. They look too awful, he said of the assembled audience, we should simply pretend we have made a mistake.

Don't be ridiculous, she said, pulling her arm away and walking serenely towards the men and women who awaited her arrival. She had thought that he would leave, and when she noticed, halfway through her reading, that he was sitting gloomily in the back row, it caused her so much discomfort that she skipped many of the passages, and took questions instead. Soon she regretted this, for it would have been easier to bury her head in her book and read on than to speak coherently about her artistic motives with him sneering in the back. It was with great relief that she found, when she raised her eyes again to the audience after the applause was over, that he was no longer there.

She returned reluctantly after dinner to his flat. He was sitting in his armchair, smoking a pipe. Somehow he reminded her of Mother Hubbard's dog. I hate you when you are performing, he said simply.

That much was clear, she replied.

Promise me you will not associate with those people anymore while you are here.

Which people?

I don't know – whoever you had dinner with – the man who introduced you as the Indian Bruce Chatwin – whatever.

You were the one who got me into this, she reminded him. You were the one who introduced me to Ramona – I will have to see her, by the way, but surely you won't mind having lunch with her.

Ramona bores the shit out of me, he said.

She is a good literary agent, she said. And you introduced us!

I rue the day, said Morgan.

She had been afraid that they would quarrel, but that did not happen, it was worse than that, the week passed with her slipping off to keep her engagements, waking every day and wondering if she should not take her bags and check into a hotel, or just ask Ramona if she might spend the rest of her stay in her flat, she had explained the situation to her over a long lunch, but then had been consumed by a sense of betrayal towards Morgan, for Ramona had nodded in sympathy, and said, he is just jealous probably, the pygmy was kind of your joint scheme, he just feels hideously left out, I guess.

Besides, said Ramona, he wrote a novel once about fifteen years ago. I couldn't find a publisher for it.

Was it good? she asked.

Not very, said Ramona.

I need to find a postcard, said Niharika, thinking it would be unbearable to hear any more, I need to find a postcard to send to my niece.

I know just where to go, said Ramona.

How about this? she said, when they were in the shop, it was of the Mad Hatter in Central Park.

This is a frightening and beautiful city, Niharika wrote on the back of it later, someday I will bring you here.

Who are you writing to? Morgan asked.

My niece, she replied.

Have you heard from Faraday, at all? he asked.

You know that I have not, she said.

I saw him last month, said Morgan suddenly.

And you didn't tell me.

He asked me not to.

Then why are you telling me now?

Because there seems to be nothing else worth saying to you, he said.

I don't know whether to believe you, she said.

Suit yourself, said Morgan.

She took a long sip of the vodka tonic she had poured herself when she came in, he had not offered to make her a drink himself.

I have changed my ticket, she said, I am leaving tomorrow.

I won't be here then, he said. Tomorrow is the day I visit my grandfather.

Where is he now? she asked.

In a home for people with Alzheimer's on Long Island.

Can I come with you? she asked.

I thought you were leaving tomorrow, he said.

I haven't actually changed my ticket yet, she confessed.

He hesitated, as if momentarily captured like her by the hope that the act of visiting his aged grandfather together might have a cleansing effect on their friendship, but then he shook his head, I don't think that would work, he said.

She felt as if she had looked up the Christmas chimney and found it stuffed with dead birds. I am so tired, she said, biting back her tears, I'd better go to bed.

I will be leaving very early, he said, so I probably won't see you. She walked into the kitchen and topped up her drink to take with her to bed. And then she tarried awhile to look among his books for something to read, and finally chose a volume of Paradise Lost which he seemed to possess in twelve slim texts, I'm going to bed now, she said.

He did not raise his head from his book. Goodbye, he said.

Goodbye, Morgan, she said.

Her last few months in Oxford were filled with the trivial details of the final composition and annotation of her thesis, but finally it was bound and submitted, and she took the opportunity to travel for a few weeks in Europe with an old friend, before the oral examination, for after that was over it was clear to her that she no longer would have any reason to remain in the country.

What are you going to do now? her aunt asked her. Will you stay in research or write another book, or both?

I am going to go home, she said, I am going back to Calcutta.

But there is nobody there, her aunt protested.

I can live on my own, she said, I am almost thirty years old.

Besides, the old cook is still there, and the gatekeeper. I will keep a few more servants.

I shiver to think of you alone in that big old house, said her aunt.

I think I will keep most of it shut up, she said, just as it is now.

And what will you do there? her aunt asked.

Just sit and think for a while, and eventually write another book, I hope.

I hate to think of you shut up like a recluse in the house, her aunt said.

Who said anything about being a recluse? All my relatives and friends are still there, not to mention the other nine million people.

Still, I cannot help feeling that you will have rather a solitary existence.

You do not have to think of it as permanent, she consoled her, it is just what I feel like doing right now, it is what I feel I must do.

She did not tell her that part of the motive for moving back to Calcutta was that she had been seized by the urge to write about her uncle, Debendranath Roy, who had now been dead for almost eighteen years. She felt that there were currents lurking within her that would help her understand the mystery of his suicide, and that these might slowly surface as she reconstructed the narrative of his existence, but that to let this happen she must return to the house where they had both lived, that they had both left to come to Oxford. Wonderful, painful things had happened to her there, whereas he had ostensibly led a very quiet life, married his landlady's niece, briefly tried to re-establish himself in Calcutta, and then returned to a teaching job in England. He had apparently been very content with his easy life, with its long vacations during which he had travelled extensively in Europe as had been his childhood dream, had been happy to spend the evenings reading and listening to music, sometimes going to the cinema, which had also been a passion in his youth, and then one day, after a delightful luncheon with his old Professor when they had discussed the pleasant possibility of his returning to research, he had decided that the only real course for him was to take his own life. She remembered the curious taste of that dawn, like some powerful but sickly sweet medication, vile with thick promise upon her young tongue, your uncle is dead, the maidservant wept, and Niharika wept with her, not out of grief, nor out of shock, but simply because tears were the only language that she knew for the terrible sense of excitement that jostled with the disbelief that she would never see her uncle again. She remembered how, on the evening before he had left their house, years before, they had transferred the lemon shaped stamps from Sierra Leone from his old collection to her new stampbook, for he had agreed to give them to her, it lay open at the page on the dining room table with even the bowl of water and the pot of paste exactly as it was when they had been called to dinner, and she had hurried to fish out the last waterlogged stamp and set it to dry upon a cracked plate. The following morning she had surveyed this tableau, that nobody had bothered yet to dismantle, with an awful sense of having been betrayed. Her grief at his death seemed pale and featureless in comparison. So he had disappeared, somehow it was almost natural that such a calamity should befall him, it was simply the last convulsion in his obviously extraordinary fate. In any case, perhaps he had not drowned at all, just been spirited away by a crafty magician to some dark and lonely castle, or seduced by aliens to accompany them back to a different galaxy, or perhaps as he rested in the shade of the willows upon the shore he had been slowly exsanguinated by a bold vampire, and now roamed the world undead. Now it was not so much what happened to him afterwards that excited her imagination as what had happened to him before, what had driven him on a beautiful spring day, so many years ago, to make sure that the boat he had hired returned without him.

It had filled her with something greater than hope when it

had suddenly become clear to her that she must devote herself to the task of reconstructing his life. It was not just something she felt would add to the inventory of her existence, but rather something she absolutely must do, and this sense of destiny had quietly exhilarated her. She had set herself down almost immediately to the practicalities of returning to her childhood home, now abandoned by all, and living there in quiet contemplation of her uncle's life. The book would have a very long gestation she knew, and she planned to savour every minute of it. She was lucky that circumstances enabled her to do so, for it would be easy to support herself financially in Calcutta. Her parents would pay for the upkeep of the house, and also for her own maintenance if she required them to do so. They still hoped perhaps that she would marry, and what they had set aside as a dowry for her – of course to be indirectly offered for the overt transaction was seen to be vulgar and regressive – would easily feed and clothe her for the rest of her life.

I do not like to think of you alone in that house, said Jennifer. In the six years that Niharika had been in Oxford, Jennifer had seen her become progressively more solitary. It had been so different in her first year, when many of the meals she cooked especially for her would go cold while she waited, until the phone rang and it was her niece apologizing once again, but would she mind terribly if she came tomorrow, her friends were really keen for her to come down to London with them, would it be all right if she went with them, and visited her tomorrow, the food would surely keep? And Jennifer would carefully wrap the dishes in clingfilm, eat what could not be reheated, although it was as likely as not that she would phone again and apologize that she already had an appointment, how could it have slipped her mind yesterday. Often she would find herself weeping as she put the food away. It was not that she felt that Niharika did not care deeply for her, it was only natural after all that she should prefer the company of her young and varied friends, but it worried Jennifer how intensely she craved her presence. Her evening could so easily be ruined by her niece not showing up for dinner. She wished that it did not hurt her so, for she felt if Niharika were to find this out she would cease to come altogether, and this would be unbearable to her, for now at least she could live in the promise of her visit for the whole day, rummage in the covered market for things she might like to eat, consult her cookbooks for the correct way to quarter a chicken, pick flowers from the garden for her to take back to her dreary college room. Sometimes she dreamed that if Niharika married one of the many young men she seemed to know so well, if she married one of them and had children, that perhaps she might be inducted into the role of a grandmother to the child, how happy she would be to take care of the baby while Niharika worked. It was not so unlikely. It seemed obvious to Jennifer that a few of them were quite in love with her, but she seemed entirely indifferent, perhaps she had someone waiting for her back in Calcutta, Jennifer had thought.

And then something had happened, that summer, or just afterwards. Perhaps the young man in Calcutta had given her up. Jennifer would never know, but she could smell upon her, as easily as the scent of bruised camomile when she walked over that patch of her lawn, she could smell upon her the anguish of love. And with it came the inclination to shun the company of those that she had cultivated so lavishly in the past year, instead she preferred to be with Jennifer, go for long silent walks through the autumn woods, or sit reading by the log effect gas fire in her living room. There were periods when she would seem strangely and intensely happy, but the core of this happiness telescoped inwards, further and further inwards, it seemed to Jennifer, until it became indistinguishable from her general reticence. She could not make sense of any of it, and was glad when Niharika announced she had decided to spend a year in America. The change would undoubtedly do her good, Jennifer felt. Indeed, when she returned, she seemed very much more energetic and full of plans, I've decided to write a novel about the pygmy, she told her.

You were always a good storyteller, said Jennifer, not knowing what else to say. She smiled as if she knew she was much more than that, and the arrogance of it was pleasing to Jennifer who had begun to fear that something was destroying Niharika's confidence in herself, something which she was sure could only be the love of a man, for what else was there to quench the fire within a woman like her, whose stern will she had known so clearly even when she was a child. She had shown her stories then that were mainly in pictures, for she did not know how to spell the many words in her head, but pictures could say as much, and more, for she could draw in a policeman where there was no policeman before, but to go back and invent a policeman in a story was more difficult, she had explained to Jennifer. And here she was now telling her that she was going to return to her childhood home, to the old mansion named Mandalay where all of this had happened long ago, to draw herself in, like her policeman, where nothing should be, and most certainly not her, it seemed to Jennifer, most certainly not her.

But what will you do there?

Sit and think for a while, perhaps, said Niharika dreamily. Would you come and visit me? she asked Jennifer.

Of course I will, said Jennifer. She mentioned a friend who was keen to travel to India, they had already been together to Turkey, and a few weeks ago they had persuaded some of their other friends to join them on a trip to Puerto Rico.

Niharika tried to imagine Jennifer and her friend in the crumbling mansion in Calcutta. If they came, it would mark a true watershed, beyond which Debendranath Roy would have become a mere memory, and the time that he and Jennifer spent in Calcutta would finally be relegated to a different epoch in all their lives. And then Jennifer, suddenly turning to her with tears in her eyes, said – I could never go back, I could never go back to Mandalay. For having Reba as a guest in her home had brought back to her in sharp detail, the pain and humiliation she had so gladly borne then for no reason except that it was the shape of things as they were, as he had wanted them, Debendranath Roy. Sometimes, she had suspected that he could never be happy anywhere else, that to leave Mandalay would be fearfully wrong, and she must do all that was within her to keep him from such a decision, which seemed so darkly imminent and which, in part, she so welcomed. To pack their bags and be gone forever, what bliss, to never have to wake and meet with Reba's disapproval – of her clothes, of her manners, of her lack of grace – a disapproval that she communicated by a simple arch of her eyebrow behind her cup of tea, a disapproval that she would often rechannel upon her children, chiding them for some trivial misdeed, her sons ignored her, but her daughter would flinch as if whipped, and Jennifer would wish she were dead.

Still, something had told her that they should not leave Mandalay, even though it was clear they would be happier elsewhere. But perhaps he would have drowned anyway, perhaps it was best that at least she had had five happy years with him in their little nest in Highgate. They had been happy years for her, to him at times they must have been unbearable, but she did not know that until he disappeared from her life, she had no inkling that the walls of their flat, which she had so lovingly painted a magnolia white, must have often closed in upon him with the insistence of a bulldozer, the pretty plantpots on the sill screeched their pinks and violets till his head rang, the avocado green of the bathtub which she polished so carefully every day must have seemed to him like a sallow grave as he filled it in the evening for his bath. How was she to have known this? How was she to have known this when, at other times, with Louis Armstrong playing on the record player that he had bought her for her birthday, and the two of them sharing a bottle of wine while they sorted through photographs of their recent holiday in Italy, the year in Calcutta had seemed like a distant nightmare, not likely to recur? How was she to have known this when the two of them would play with a friend's child that they had offered to look after for the morning, and she would feel as he crept around the room with the urchin screaming with delight upon his back, that soon he would not be able to so fervently resist the thought of having his own children, that they would finally be a family, send pictures of their children to Calcutta, for by then he would have been reconciled with his father surely, or so she hoped. It was true there were times when her company seemed painful to him, but she had thought that this did not apply specifically to herself, just that he needed, like all men, to be alone. On the day before he died, she had bought him a painting of the angel Gabriel as a birthday present. For many days after it stood by the door with its face to the wall, and sometimes she had the pointless urge to go and turn it around and try and understand why it was that he had so violently disliked it.

How could you have bought this for me? he had asked her, you know how particular my tastes are.

But I thought you liked religious paintings, she had said, tears streaming down her cheeks.

Because I was watching that programme on Russian icons? he had asked.

I am sorry, she had said, wiping her eyes on her cardigan sleeve.

Sometimes I wish I could lie to you, said Debendranath Roy.

A ten-year-old nephew of hers had been visiting them for the day, they were to take him to the zoo that afternoon. He had helped her choose the painting from the kerbside stall that morning, and now, confused by their strange interchange, was playing quietly with his food. She remembered how sadly he looked across the table at the boy, desperately moulding landscapes out of his fishfingers and mash, and then turned his eyes towards the garden, where the grass, unnaturally long for that time of the year, writhed with an alien grace. Then he had turned to face her once again, it does not matter, he had tried to say with kindness, it does not matter at all. Going to the zoo can be my birthday present, he had added gaily. He smiled a strange smile, and left the table saying he was going to try and put something on paper for his appointment with Professor Faraday the following day. She had wiped her eyes and slowly wrapped the painting back up in its brown paper covering. I am sure you will be able to return it, her nephew had tried to console her.

Besides he might like it if he looks at it again, the boy had said hopefully.

She had squeezed him tight. You are a very sweet boy, she had told him, but your uncle is right, it will not go with the striped wallpaper in his study.

His study was the only room she had not tried to paint. It was his retreat, the tiny shoebox of a room, crammed with his books and papers, she had not dared move them aside so that she could decorate the room. Why does he have to hang it in his study? the boy had asked.

Never mind, she had said. Would you like an ice cream for your pudding?

Oh yes, the boy had nodded, relieved at finally being able to disengage himself from the topic of the painting.

The trip to the zoo had been extremely pleasant. It was a bright spring day, and Debendranath Roy had entertained the boy with stories of elephants and tigers in his native land. They had had a big tea afterwards, and large chocolate milkshakes as a special treat. After his parents had taken him away that evening, Debendranath Roy had apologized to her for reacting so strongly against the painting in front of the boy, I was not thinking, he had admitted.

You do not have to try so hard to make me happy, he had told her. You are best exactly as you are.

And then he had excused himself saying that he needed a long sleep, to be refreshed for his trip to Oxford on the following day, and she had sat down in front of the television with her knitting, secure that the crisis over the painting had dissolved. She worked late into the night, intent on finishing the pullover that she was making for him so that, if he wanted, he could wear it to Oxford the next day. She pulled the last stitch tight as the clock chimed three, and then finally took herself to bed. When she woke in the morning, he had left already, for it was almost ten o'clock, the pullover lay stretched across the baseboard of the bed where she had left it.

No, she could never go back to Mandalay again, it would be like peeling the scabs off all her old wounds. She could not expose herself to the memories of the helplessness that she had felt in the year that she had lived there, at the mercy of the heat and the tropical germs, and the scalding looks of her sister-in-law as she wandered in from a trip to New Market with her hair clinging in wet fury to her forehead, her dress hanging loosely off her sunburnt shoulder, showing a nylon brassiere strap surrounded by a fan of white fingers upon her red flesh where other straps had rested. You need a shower, Reba would suggest almost solicitously, but it would be painfully clear to Jennifer that all she wanted was for her to be gone, and the grace of her luncheon with her children restored.

What had hurt her most though was when at a party after a school play Niharika had quite subtly denied her presence, running to join her friends whenever Jennifer came near, tossing away her compliments with a shake of her head. It seemed as if she was ashamed of her, and later she realized from the way that some of the other children looked at her that it was the length of her dress that was the cause of the child's embarrassment. She was terrified that her friends would tease her about it later, or worse still giggle behind her back. When the time came to leave, Niharika ignored her almost entirely, holding tightly onto her mother's hand, climbing into her rickshaw rather than Jennifer's, which she had never done before when presented with the choice, and sitting upon the crooked cushions of her rickshaw alone, Jennifer felt that her heart would break. What had made her pick out this flowery little number, what but the fact that she had paid such an absurdly high price for it last summer when she had met her sister to go shopping together for a last time in London. She had convinced Jennifer to splash out on the dress, treat yourself for once, she had urged her, for once do something for yourself. After she returned from India, her sister would come and see her sometimes in London, convince her to go shopping, or to get an expensive haircut. Once she persuaded her to get a 'complete make-over' and she had returned to their flat in Highgate heavily burnished, with an array of cosmetics jingling in her bag. They had cost her almost a week's salary – it is worth it, her sister had told her, you will feel like a new person. And indeed there was a certain transformation in her attitude as she entered the flat and found him grumbling that he was hungry, why had she not cooked supper? He did not seem to notice that she looked any different, and for the first time in her life she actually threw down her shopping bags and asked him to get his own fish and chips for a change. And he had looked up at her in surprise, risen from his chair, and put on his overcoat to go to the chip shop. Shall I get some for you? he had asked.

I am not hungry, she had replied, swallowing back her tears. And then she had washed her face in the kitchen sink with fairy liquid as she finished doing the dishes, and decided that whatever confidence came with a newly painted face was not for her. She had been happy when he came back to share his chips. The plates taste of lipstick, he had teased her, what has your sister put you up to now?

Do you think I should wear make-up? she had asked.

That is entirely your decison, he had replied.

She had never touched again the cosmetics she had bought that day, and finally she had exchanged them with her sister for a large brimmed straw hat, for they were invited to a garden party at Debendranath Roy's Oxford college, and her sister told her she must wear a summer hat. She had decorated it with a green ribbon to match her dress, and he had been pleased by the effect, he had presented her happily to his old mentor, Nicholas Faraday, and his stately wife, Rosemary, who had taken her arm at once and led her into a large tent where they were serving strawberries and cream. Come and meet my son Daniel, she had said.

Daniel was powdering his strawberries with sugar when they found him. He was an undergraduate at Cambridge, she was told, important for them to get away, his mother had explained, as if one Oxbridge university was the furthest point from the other in their universe, Daniel was studying architecture. He looked at her with his splendid blue eyes, and there was something so candid in his glance that she felt her cheeks grow a little warm. I like the green ribbon, he said with youthful arrogance, and then proceeded to langourously lick the cream off his fingers.

Get us some strawberries, ordered his mother, and no cream or sugar for me please.

I have already got you some, he said, producing a dish of bald fruit. You can have this one, he said to Jennifer, offering her his own, and then he disappeared into the crowd to procure some for himself.

She did not see him again until many years later when she had come back to live in Oxford, converted the old boarding house into a Bed & Breakfast with central heating and hot showers in every room, she did not see him until she had been adopted in her widowhood by the Faradays, and they took her one evening to an opening of an exhibition of Daniel's photographs in London. They were all of women in various states of subtle humiliation, walking on tiptoe with one heel fallen off an absurdly high pair of shoes, painting a chapped pair of lips by their reflection in a powder compact mirror on an underground platform, being led home in tears by a fat and irate man who one could only assume to be a husband. Jennifer had wondered whether he deeply despised women to present them like this, but then he was so charming to her and all the other women that she saw him with, and besides he had with him his girlfriend, Alison, who was tall and imposing, and so full of confidence that the subjects of his photographs looked even more tawdry beside her. Jennifer was interested to see, in the reviews of his work that she came across in the weeks that followed, that he was criticized for being disrespectful to women, denegrating what should be humbly celebrated in a woman's life, those odd moments of embarrassment, their own small attempts at making their lives less unbearable, it appeared to the critics that he was mocking rather than glorifying the little woman's tragedy, and that did not go down well at all in the artistic circles of the early eighties. And so Daniel Faraday gave up art, and began to take photographs instead for money, and in a few years had established himself as a leading commercial photographer. He married Alison, whose career was also taking off in the city, moved into a tall Georgian townhouse in Notting Hill Gate, and soon had enough extra time upon his hands to promise Alison that if they had a child, he would take the main responsibility of its nurture, of course with the help of a nanny. She found the proposition acceptable, and sailed through her pregnancy and early weeks of motherhood with unusual ease. She refused however, on any account, to go through it again. Their son would be an only child, but that was not such a bad thing. Sometimes, Jennifer would go and babysit in Stanton St John. He was a lovely baby, she longed so much for a child of her own, even wondered whether she should try and find someone to have one with, now that over ten years had passed since Debendranath Roy disappeared. Soon it would be too late to have children at all. Later that year, she bumped into her old friend Tom, he was still in the building trade, and divorced now from his wife. It seemed that he was still interested in her, and for a while she managed to convince herself that perhaps she had all along been meant for him, that the episode with Debendranath Roy had just been a very long diversion from the true course of her life, but then the news arrived that Niharika was coming to Oxford, and Tom suddenly shrunk into a paunchy middle-aged builder whom she could not possibly love.

Niharika had arrived in Oxford and pinned her again onto the strange landscape where there was a river that had taken away her husband and a house in the distance where they had once lived, and then beneath the trees to one side a wealth of sweet memories of their five years in London, this was the lay of the land that she inhabited, how could she have thought of deserting it? Niharika had arrived and all thought of beginning a new life had left her, the desire had reassembled within her to embrace and cherish the past, but now Niharika was leaving again, perhaps she would come back, but if she did not, Jennifer felt sure that she was not likely to see any of her husband's family again. Her brother-in-law was now too frail to travel regularly, so she could no longer expect the occasional telephone call from London, his sons hardly remembered her, there was no one else.

Rosemary Faraday came to help her pack her things – anything you do not want, put in these bags, and I'll take them over to Oxfam, she said.

It is awfully kind of you to offer to help, Niharika said.

Not at all, she replied, I enjoy putting people's lives in order. I always used to itch to sort out Daniel's things, but he never let me of course, and now he has the capable Alison organizing his life.

She found it hard to imagine that anyone might be organizing Daniel's life, but perhaps it was true that his wife saw to it that his shirts were ironed and that his sock drawer was always freshly stocked. How would she have performed in that capacity, she wondered, certainly not with the same skill. Managing a household was a talent she had not inherited from her mother, even her own limited affairs were in sad disarray as she had realized while attempting to wind them all up before she left. She had also discovered within herself recently a strange compulsion to throw things away, to assess their value almost immediately, be it a letter, or a set of coffee cups, she felt a keen pleasure in discarding any item that she did not judge to be of significance. It was only a mild mania, and it did mean there was far less to sort through now than there might have been otherwise. There was a time though when she had treasured many trivial things, the miniature salt and pepper containers that her father brought back from his aeroplane journeys, a piece of earthenware that someone had told her had archaelogical value, a set of pearly shark's teeth that a man had sold her on the seashore in Puri, a painted papier mache egg that she had found in a railway carriage, these and other motley treasures she stowed in an old shoebox and kept under her bed, no one was allowed to touch it.

It was Morgan who had weaned her from her attachment to small objects. He had showed her once what was his one and only treasure, a locket with a lyre in it made of the hairs of Keats' head. His father had paid a very large sum of money for it once, and because he had expressed an interest in it, had given it to him, hoping that it might cure him of his general apathy, his total lack of interest in all their other assets. He kept it in a small box beside his bedside table, and told her that when he could not sleep he would take it out and look at it, he did not know why it meant so much to him. It was not just because he cared so much for Keat's poetry. Here were his hairs wrought into the delicate shape of a lyre, why did they matter more than the hairs of someone who had not left the world so many of his thoughts and dreams. It kept him entertained to muse upon whether the object would lose its value for him if the hairs were found not to belong to Keats. A geneticist that he knew had told him that the techniques were available now to ascertain this conclusively, and it cheered Morgan to think that it could not be done without destroying the fine craftsmanship, perhaps it was the sheer beauty of it that appealed to him, perhaps it had nothing to do with Keats at all.

She had only seen it once, and the trace of thin lines had so enraptured her that Morgan had almost looked worried that she might ask him if he would give it to her, a request that he would not have been able to refuse. But she only sighed deeply and handed it back to him. He had not dared to show it to her again, and since the event all material things had seemed somehow diminished, just as being with Daniel Faraday had once so devalued all other human interaction and made her so guardful of her own company. Sometimes, she dreamt that Morgan had sent her the locket as a gesture of reconciliation, but it never happened. No word arrived from him, let alone a gift. She felt she had lost him forever, and the pain of it was like missing a limb. At least Daniel's absence left her whole, in that perfect completeness of separation from a lover, the honeyed anguish that she had celebrated in the words of the poet long before she knew its sharp bite: *your absence sweetens the thirst for you that fills me on this night of full moon, what exquisite mirages the moonlight conjures upon my closed lids*, it was with a terrible wistfulness that she had sung this at a gathering in a friend's house a few days before she had left Calcutta, for at the time she had wished that she had someone to leave behind, someone whose thoughts she might hold against her lips as she wandered on misty nights among the spires of Oxford. She had been twenty-three years old and love in none of its guises had come her way. It seemed unlikely that it would find her in a foreign land, and never did she imagine that it would come in the shape of Daniel Faraday, the last man to have ever seen her uncle alive.

SAFFRON

That night he dreamt that he was at the gates of Mandalay again, but though he shook them hard they would not open for they were hung with a great rusty lock, and all the while the gatekeeper stood watching him, shaking his head, I cannot let you in, said the gatekeeper, I cannot let you in, and it is not just because I threw away the key to that lock a long time ago, but because you are dead, said the gatekeeper, you are dead, Debendranath Roy.

It was I who took them the telegram, said the gatekeeper, they were having their evening meal, your father, your brother, his wife, and the children. At the prow of that great table they were crowded, eating their mutton curry. I gave the telegram to your brother, and trembling, stood by. Telegrams had never brought good news in this family. He is feared drowned, your brother said bewildered, Deben has drowned, he said, looking helplessly around at his father, his wife, his three children.

You have been dead for many years, Debendranath Roy, said the old gatekeeper, one by one you have all disappeared, leaving me to guard this arthritic house alone, this house once so grand, now like a broken hive, humming with old grains of honey. Nobody lives here anymore, and yet I let my old wife shiver in our shack rather than trespass upon its decay. I dare not move her into the house, even though the boundaries that were once so real are now simply like a skin of milk stretched across the swing doors.

But I am here now, he protested, do you think me a ghost then?

You are not a ghost, admits the gatekeeper, I have become intimate with ghosts, very intimate with ghosts, over these long years.

I have been here longer than any of you, said the gatekeeper, for I came in the year that your father married. I was recruited from your mother's household in North Bengal to accompany her to her new home, to guard her as she made the strange journey to this city, with so many expectations, none of which were ever fulfilled. Do you think they will let me go on to a university? she had asked me, poor ignorant me, a peasant boy from her village, do you think they will let me carry on to university? she had asked me feverishly.

My mother?

Your mother.

I have not thought of her for so long.

You have been dead for many years, Debendranath Roy, said the old gatekeeper, and now you have come back, not as a ghost, but in the flesh.

Indeed I have, he said, and I am in dire need of a bath.

But I cannot let you in, said the gatekeeper.

He wakes to the scrape of an aluminium kettle against the metal edge of his berth as the train jerks into motion and the young tea vendor who has just climbed into their carriage loses his balance. Luckily he is not scalded, the damage is limited to a few disposable cups of unglazed earthenware that Debendranath Roy itches to put back together even though he knows that they would be of no use to anybody. I will give you some money for the cups, he tells the boy. Sir, you are kind, the boy replies, it is not much, but then I earn so little, I can hardly afford to lose even these.

As the train approaches Calcutta, and the morning becomes more bright, it crowds with commuters who have missed their local trains, and with hawkers of every description, for whom Debendranath Roy feels an intense sympathy, not so much because of the wretchedness of their condition, but because, like him, they too seem to be trying to eke out a living from the surreal. When he disembarks at Howrah station, his pockets are stuffed with their wares, bottles of stain-removing liquid, packets of rubberbands, a corked test tube full of needles of various lengths and thicknesses.

Outside the station, he takes a bus that is obviously going to the Esplanade, and from there it is only a short walk to his childhood home, to the house that they never called by its name. But he cannot bring himself to make the journey straight away, instead he wanders into the Grand Hotel, and has a beer by the pool, it is noon, he had thought he might be there by now, that the gatekeeper's wife would be cooking him lunch, but something is holding him back, something tells him he must wait until the frantic rhythm of a tropical morning has fully ceased, and the slow tempo of the afternoon has firmly established itself, for he senses that something awaits him in Mandalay beyond the repose that he seeks.

He finds himself loitering in the bookshop in the Grand Hotel Arcade. It is more of an overflowing bookstall, but here he has browsed for hours as a student, jostled by other eager readers, it was here that he came like a hungry dog in the hope that he would be able to fill the huge gaps in his knowledge of politics and history that had yawned so wide in those wonderful evenings at Reba's father's house, when he would sit enthralled but tongueless in the winds of a fierce and splendid debate, and wish that he had at least a few choice words to offer, especially if, as was often so, she was there, at her father's feet, quietly voicing her own opinions, that he ached to endorse with an especially coruscating comment. But he could usually only come up with some tangential observation from the physical sciences that would cause them to pause and think but then quickly replunge into the flow of their discourse, so that sometimes he would feel as if he had interrupted, albeit with applause, the rehearsal of a dedicated group of performing artists.

He finds a book on Bohemian glass, and leafs gladly through it, until the bookseller reminds him of the price – you can of course pay in instalments, he says. Yes, I know, says Debendra-nath Roy, but it still may not be something that I can afford.

Actually, you still owe me some money, says the man. Debendranath Roy looks up at him where he sits high above a mound of books. It is the same person with whom he had an account in his youth and afterwards. Was it true that he had left the city twenty-five years ago without settling up, it had never crossed his mind.

I am terribly sorry, he says. Can I pay you now?

It is no matter, says the bookseller. The sum would be worth nothing now anyway, unless I calculated the inflation.

You could have sent a bill to my father, says Debendranath Roy.

I thought you would come back, says the bookseller, but then they said you had drowned.

There was some truth in that, says Debendranath Roy.

And then onwards through the network of backstreets that had always been his route back home, when he would hurry along with his new books swinging in his satchel, already savouring the hours he would spend in their company. He takes the same route now, clutching his old suitcase and with the book on Bohemian glass wrapped neatly in brown paper and string, but the streets have changed, the grave old shopsigns are gone and in their place are pieces of backlit plastic. The shop windows no longer announce their wares in sparse dusty dignity, instead the sunlight festers upon rows of gleaming imitations of goods that irrationally bear unmagical allusions to foreign cities and brandnames upon their faces, he shrinks back from them and hurries on.

Finally, the gates of Mandalay appear, thick with rust and not tightly barred as in his recurrent dream, but slightly ajar, with a young girl kneeling by them and trying to coax a kitten to enter through the opening by offering the creature a saucer of milk. The kitten, too young and confused to seize this opportunity of a lifetime, stands in a trance outside the gates, until Debendranath Roy kneels down to stroke it and it jerks

130

alive and runs away. The girl lets out a wail, there now you've spoilt everything, she says.

She will come back, says Debendranath Roy.

Who are you anyway? she asks, for her childish intuition tells her that he is no stranger to these premises.

I think I am your grandfather's brother, he replies.

The one that drowned long long ago?

I did not drown, he says.

But you did, says a voice behind her, and Debendranath Roy looks up to meet the eyes of his niece, Niharika. We were having our evening meal when the telegram arrived, she says, my grandfather, my father, my mother, my twin brothers and I. The gatekeeper gave the telegram to my father, and trembling, stood by, as my father announced, he is feared drowned, my father said, Deben has drowned, he said, looking helplessly around at his father, his wife, his twin sons and myself, his daughter.

What are you doing here? he asks.

I have been living here for the last two years, she replies. The child, she explains, is the daughter of the elder of her twin brothers.

I know, he replies.

Have you been watching us? she asks. All these years, have you been watching us?

Not closely, he says. But a few years ago they all came for a holiday to the hill station where I have been hiding all these years. I was sitting in peace in the teashop where I often ate my breakfast, drinking tea and looking through a book of crosswords, when who should walk in but my brother, but he did not see me, perhaps he would not have recognized me anyway.

He thinks you are dead, she reminds him.

I followed him back to their hotel, and then, I will admit I watched them, for the week that remained of their stay, I shamelessly spied on them, and I learnt much of what had passed in the time that I had been gone. I learnt that this house had been empty for many years, that your parents lived in Delhi, with your brother and his wife and the beautiful children who played upon the hotel lawn. I saw her – he says, turning to the child who has managed to attract the attention once more of the scrawny kitten – thought I might try and talk to her, says Debendranath Roy, but I didn't want to feel that she was lonely enough to want to talk to a stranger.

She wrote to me from there, says Niharika, and told there was a detective in dark glasses prowling the grounds.

Then she did see me, he says with a small laugh. No one else noticed, I don't think, it was so easy to eavesdrop, and such fun to piece together the fragments of their conversation into a picture of the present. They spoke of you, I am afraid with as much anxiety as with pride, and I was thrilled to know that the book that I had found by a woman of your name was indeed yours and not by someone else with your credentials, for I only ever came across a paperback that had no picture of you on its cover.

And you would have known it was me from my picture?

I think so, he says and smiles. He had found a copy of her novel in the Teaplanter's Club at the hill station where he had hidden himself since his drowning. He saw the book, flung carelessly upon a pingpong table, and after the initial shock of identifying her as the author, his heart had swelled with a strange pride that he almost felt he had no right to feel, he had asked the teaplanters if he could borrow the book, and one of them had taken it out for him in his name. While he read it, he felt, although it was so far removed from anything he could ever have imagined, he felt that it could only have been written by someone of his own flesh, no one but she, he felt, could have written that book. He sat out upon his veranda, and read all night, and his heart filled with gratitude, not to her, but to the chain of events that had conspired to create such a thing, a thing of beauty that he could somehow see as part of himself.

But tell me why you have been living here, he says. That is not what I expected at all.

I have been writing a book about you, she says.

Is it finished?

It is, she replies. It should be on the bookshelves within a few weeks.

I am glad to hear that, for if it was not I would have regretted that I had come.

You think that this sudden subversion of your personal history would have any effect on my narrative?

I am sure it has its own life, he acknowledges humbly, but I am glad to have appeared after it has been completed. I should very much like to read it, he adds.

That I could not prevent, even if I wanted to.

If you do not want me to read it, I swear I will not.

Your oaths have little meaning, says his niece.

He hears the gate creak behind him. It is the gatekeeper with a bag of vegetables. I could only find some old aubergines, he explains to his young mistress.

Look who is here, she says.

It cannot be, says the gatekeeper inspecting him, it cannot be.

I did not drown, he explains.

I never really believed it, confesses the gatekeeper.

Well, here I am, says Debendranath Roy.

The gatekeeper takes his suitcase and leads the way into the house, the portico stairs are chipped now in many places, and the floor of the broad veranda is dull and cracked, the swing doors groan as they enter. Inside it is barer than he ever remembers. I got rid of the carpets, explains Niharika, they were filthy and threadbare, and the marble floors are so much cooler in this heat.

And most of the furniture?

I put it away, she says.

What remains has been recovered in raw canvas, the effect is not disagreeable to him. At one end of the room is a low platform, covered in embroidered quilts, upon which repose many of her mother's old musical instruments, I am learning to play the sitar, says Niharika, even though it is of course too late for me to learn to play anything.

It is not too late, he consoles her. Since disappearing from your lives, I have mastered the flute, I do not claim to play well, but certainly well enough for my own pleasure, which must be your goal as well.

But you were able to reinvent yourself entirely, she says. That must have given you a different sort of energy.

But why are you here then if not to find a life that does not call for you to lie at each instant? Surely, you are here for the same purpose that I ostensibly left this world twenty years ago?

I had not thought of it that way, she says.

Can you be sure? he asks.

I was not planning to stay for much longer, she confesses. In another two weeks, I return to Oxford on a year's creative writing fellowship, and after that I do not know.

They follow the gatekeeper to Debendranath Roy's old room, not the one he occupied in the year that he lived here as a married man, for she has been using that as a study. It seems strangely logical that he should want to return to the room where he spent his boyhood and youth. A rusty lock hangs upon the door, but the gatekeeper produces a set of keys from his pocket and finds the right one without much hesitation, for he is a man of method. Without him this great house would have been consumed by disorder long before it fell into decay.

Inside it is velvet with dust, and the few gaps in the shutters are like wounds bleeding tropical sunlight, I will send someone to clean the place immediately, says the gatekeeper, she can do it while you have lunch.

I would have liked a bath first, says Debendranath Roy.

I will send up some water then, says the gatekeeper.

None of the plumbing works anymore, explains Niharika.

Indeed the showerhead is caked in limecrust in the bathroom that he is told to use, it wobbles dangerously as he reaches to touch it, he tips the metal bucket high above his head with the grace of an executioner and dries himself with the old thin towels that the gatekeeper has laid out, they smell of napthalene which is oddly comforting to him, and after drying himself, he feels happier, as if they might have soaked up some of the darker exudates of his soul.

Lunch is served at the old dining table, the three of them sit together at one end, humbled by its expanse, and he remembers a time when he was just a boy and the table was always crowded with men, his father and brother of course, and various visiting cousins, but also men that worked for them, if they had come in the evening to discuss some urgent matter as they often did, when they would be urged to stay and eat. Meals were prepared in those days for an indefinite number of diners, and still sometimes the womenfolk and the servants would have to make do with boiled eggs and potatoes, laced with mustard oil and chillies, which was exactly how he had fed himself to start with, although now he is a reasonably good cook, he tells them.

Can you make tandoori chicken? his brother's granddaughter asks.

If you provide me with a tandoor oven, and the right spices, he replies.

My grandmother makes wonderful tandoori chicken, and she doesn't have a tandoori oven, boasts the girl.

Your grandmother can do strange and wonderful things, he says.

It seems oddly easy to call her so – your grandmother – the woman who was his reason to live and his reason to die, whose every action and every word had echoed within him incessantly until suddenly one day, a few years ago, he had woken without any thoughts of her, and found that they did not come during the day either, a day which was white and empty otherwise, and should have been devoted to the perfect contemplation of her, remained free of any trace of her, and yet was just as pure and pleasant, and Debendranath Roy had realized that he was truly beyond loving her now, that the ordeal by fire had ended, he was free to go, but where? where but here, in this sweet sunlight, and the slow drama of sibilant birdcall, where else?

My mother is a very creative cook, even in Jennifer's kitchen she managed to produce some extraordinary meals, says Niharika.

You mean in the old boarding house? he asks, suddenly trembling a little.

Did you know that she had turned it into a Bed & Breakfast?

I gathered that she had inherited it, and was running it, but they did not talk much of her.

No, of course not, she says bitterly.

But your mother stayed there when she visited you?

Does that surprise you? she asks.

But he is not listening, she realizes, he is not listening at all. He is trying to imagine her, Reba, framed in that same narrow doorway, where he had stood thirty years ago with his mighty trunk, dying of love for her, inhaling the smells of boiled beef and braised cabbage, struggling to accept that this, indeed this, was the shape of things to come.

He sees her in the narrow living room with its log effect gas fire and the plaster ceiling rose. He imagines that she might have kept her overcoat on, for it was never warm enough when he lived there. He can see her more easily at the formica-top dining table, drinking tea. Her hands are gloved in his image of her, he sees her in a state of detachment, insulated from her surroundings. He cannot envisage her cooking in the kitchen where Jennifer had once helped her aunt serve the boarders their greasy breakfasts, and where now she warms up her single portion of steak and kidney pie. It still breaks his heart to think of Jennifer in her loneliness, and yet he has never wished to think of her living in suburban contentment with another man. It would not make him much happier to know that she had built a different life without him, for he cannot think of such a life except as wholly ordinary, and for some reason it does not feel right that she, even she, should have an ordinary life.

Does English food still taste as atrocious as it did twenty years ago? he asks his niece.

I'm sure you formed a very poor opinion of English food from your boarding house meals, she replies. Jennifer has described to her what they used to eat, with some nostalgia mingled in the disbelief that they ever ate that way, for no one she knew ever ate such things any more, she herself had found that she could easily approximate a Thai curry or a Mexican bean stew with the help of the sauces and potions that called to her so seductively from the supermarket shelves. Even Reba had enjoyed the meals she had prepared for them, and only a few times asked to cook dinner herself, and on those occasions, Jennifer had realized that cooking was an art that she could never hope to master as she sat down to the simple meal of lentils and lamb curry, and was drowned, like everyone else at the table, in a host of heavenly flavours.

I hear, says Debendranath Roy, that they have become more international in their tastes, that every other restaurant is a Curry House or a Mongolian Wok Bar.

Sadly, yes.

I agree it is pity, even though I never found anything in English cuisine to commend it, says Debendranath Roy.

She remembers a hot afternoon in the summer of her first year in Oxford, another lunch at the Faraday's cottage in Stanton St John, Daniel had been there with his son, and later as the two of them sat in the shade of a broad oak beside the herb garden, he had suggested that she close her eyes and he would place a little of each herb in turn upon her tongue, so that she might start to appreciate the subtle flavours upon which European cuisine was built, and so she had chewed her way blindfolded through tarragon and parsley and the feathery leaves of fennel, he had spiked her tongue with rosemary, and soothed it with sorrel, basil was best, she felt, there was nothing quite like bruised basil, poised in nectareous perfection between the medicinal and the magical, and so with her mouth sluiced green by its juices, she had finally opened her eyes and thought how much she would like to kiss him, as he flicked the herb fragments off his hands, and looked at her in holy desperation, while his mother's voice floated down the garden calling them in for a glass of elderflower cordial.

I am awfully tired, says Debendranath Roy, with a deep yawn. Do you know if my room is ready yet?

I believe it is, she says.

Then will you excuse me? I feel I will fall asleep with my head in the chutney. The child laughs in delight at this idea, you would have to wash your hair afterwards, she observes.

Well, exactly. So I'd better go and lie down, he says, rising from his seat.

We have to go to a wedding this evening, says Niharika. We will be leaving soon, because it is some distance out of Calcutta and will take a good three hours to reach.

Who is getting married? he asks.

She names a nephew, the second of his youngest sister's children, whom he remembers to be just slightly younger than Niharika.

Why so far away?

It is where her family comes from. She is a girl who works in the same office. She has been commuting in every day from this mofussil town, her family are not well off. Everyone, needless to say, was violently opposed to the match, which is partly why I am so keen to go.

He takes in this information, his hands still firm upon the shoulders of his dining chair.

Let it not tempt you, says his niece, to come as a ghost to this wedding feast, for the situation is tense enough as it is.

I would not think of it, he says. After all, I am not invited.

You did not leave us with an address when you drowned, says his niece.

Debendranath Roy notices suddenly that the sky has

darkened ominously. It is going to rain, he observes. I hope this will not make your journey even more unpleasant.

The car is airconditioned, she says. We can seal ourselves off from everything, the rain, the heat, the mud, the oil fumes, the dung smoke – I would not take the girl otherwise. She is not used to such things.

In his room, there are clean sheets upon his bed, but the pillowcases smell of mothballs and mildew, they have probably been lying in an old linen chest for years, he closes his eyes and tries to sleep, but the shutters are flapping in the sudden wind, and soon the rain comes lashing down, and instead of sleeping, he gets up and walks over to watch the rain in the cemetery beside their house, visible only from the window of his bedroom. He remembers how he had once, in the peak of his desperation, climbed over the gates to be among the moonlit gravestones, where the pain of loving her might be eclipsed by the memory of the terror he had felt as a child at the thought of being there alone at night. And later, in the year that he had spent here with Jennifer, he had taken her for a walk there sometimes, knowing full well that the place filled her with great sorrow. But sorrow suited Jennifer, so he felt, that pale under the tall trees, trembling at the fate of some English child who had succumbed to the tropical climate in his ninth year, she was almost part of its mystery. He could learn to love her in this condition, as a phantom who had risen from the graveyard beside his window, one of the unhappy English-women who had been buried here a hundred years ago. Sometimes he had come to the cemetery with Niharika. It had been one of her favourite places. She loved to make-up stories about the people that were buried there, even though she could hardly read their names. One of them, she told him, had lived in the very house that they now called Mandalay, and had been drowned in her bath by her ugly sister. For a child of six she had a truly ghastly imagination, he had thought. And when she had an idea, she did not, like other children he knew, let it go, instead she would embellish it gradually until it grew so heavy it toppled off on its own. Later that day, she had dragged him into the junkroom where she liked to play, and pointing to the old cast iron bathtub in the corner, she had told him that this was the very tub where the the lady had been drowned by her ugly sister whose feet were too large to fit into the shoe that would have made her queen. Queen of where? he had asked wickedly. Oh anywhere, she had answered crossly, realizing that he was not taking her seriously at all.

He begins to wonder why it is that she has not been overwhelmed by his sudden appearance, his niece Niharika, the last person that he expected to find in this house. She has cloistered herself here to write about him. Could it be that in reconstructing his life's story she had reached the conclusion, long before he did, that he would return on a hot summer day to his childhood home, twenty years after he had been given up for dead? He has become accustomed to the luxury of absolutely no one knowing that he is alive, and now he feels slightly suffocated by the thought that she might have delved deeper than himself into his history, known better than himself whether he was alive or dead.

The child waves to the gatekeeper as he closes the gates after them. She is excited about the wedding, and the long journey through the outskirts of Calcutta and the grimy string of small industrial towns they will have to traverse on their way to the bride's house. The gatekeeper returns to his small gatehouse, and there he is seized by a subtle torpor as the sounds of the rain slowly cease, the clinking of pails, the slap of wet sandals, the frantic chirping of sparrows, all fade slowly under the richness of the sun which rises high and proud over the tops of the cemetery trees. His eyes do not close but his senses dim, and he is transported as he never has been before into a time long before any of this, a time long before his fate became entwined with the peculiar destiny of this family, a time simple and clean like the waters of a small stream, when he lived with his family in North Bengal. He dreams he is watching over the child Neerupama, he dreams he is watching her as she sleeps, her head upon her schoolbooks, curled up on a reed mat in a corner of the courtyard, he is waiting on his small knees for her to wake, for she has promised to teach him to read, little servant boy, why should he not know his letters? her mother has asked her, why don't you teach him to read? and she has agreed, that when he has run his errands and after she has finished her homework, she will teach him from her books, if he is a good boy, and does as he is told.

He dreams that she sleeps, her lips faintly parted, her head upon her schoolbooks, and that he is watching her, and that for the first time in his life a sense of beauty has been kindled within him by this seven year old girl, his master's favourite daughter, Neerupama. He gazes upon the curve of her brow, beaded with small drops of perspiration, and fights back a desire to wipe them away, to smooth her flesh as the clay that he has watched the craftsmen mould upon the straw frames of idols. Suddenly she opens her eyes and glares at him. Why are you staring at me? she asks.

You promised to teach me to read, he mumbles.

It is too hot now, she says.

He gets up slowly and begins to head towards the courtyard door.

Bring me a glass of water, she commands.

He turns and makes his way to the kitchen, tilts the heavy earthenware pitcher to pour her a glass of water, brings it to her where she sits, upon the grass mat, in her white frock, blinking in the heavy sunlight. She drinks greedily, holding the bell metal tumbler in both hands, wipes her mouth and says, fetch that book, over there, under the stool.

Copy these letters, she tells him, opening it to the first page. These are the vowels, all twelve of them, later I will tell you what each sounds like. Wake me up when you have finished, she says, rolling away upon her mat towards her sister, sleeping soundly beside her.

But none of it comes easily to him, and his mind begins to

wander. He thinks of the green fields where he might be wandering this very moment with his mongrel dog, he feels the wideness of the afternoon wrapping itself about him, and pulling him away. He sits and chews his pencil, and sighs in relief when a knock is heard upon the door, and a crowd of neighbours spill into the courtyard, and he is sent off to fetch savouries for their afternoon tea.

She tried again to teach him the alphabet on a few other occasions, but his head would always begin to froth with a thousand other possibilities as she set the letters before him, carved wooden pieces that their father had brought home from the big city for his sons. He liked to feel their shapes, but they never stayed with him any longer than the memory of the taste of some delicious sweetmeat that he might try and reconjure later upon his tongue, and she was impatient with him, called him a dunce, mocked his handwriting, and then before he knew it she was no longer a child but a young woman, and he still the illiterate servant boy, and the gulf between screaming wide like a wounded animal from which they could only avert their eyes. From afar he worshipped her, and yet she began to notice him less and less, regard him every day as more of a household fixture. And then suddenly she was married to a man wealthy beyond all belief, and he was sent with her to her new home, and so had returned again to focus as the only fragment of her beloved home that she had brought with her to Calcutta. For some years he basked in the complicity of this new arrangement, he was her only ally, he would bring her the letters that came thickly from her sister and mother. Before her mother-in-law set eyes upon them, he would pluck them straight from the postman's hand to deliver to her, so that she might lock herself in the bathroom to read them and weep with homesickness. He was proud to have thought of this strategy himself, she had not had to ask him this favour. He had observed her discomfort on the first day that her mother-in-law had brought her a letter from her family, stood by her as she opened it, asking her what the news was, had they found

142

a groom yet for her sister? was her brother's arm healed yet from his fall? were the mangoes ripe enough yet for eating? And two days later when another letter had arrived, her mother-in-law had sniffed and remarked that she would have thought a family of their means might be more prudent about spending money on postage, and he had seen her tears gather in her eyes, and from then on he had brought her the letters himself, and she had written to her family to instruct them to write a few lines to her in the letters that were addressed directly to her mother-in-law, to avert suspicion. After she had read them, she would slip them back to him to throw in the pond, for she did not dare keep them around the house, although once or twice she had hidden them in her textbooks, and he had watched her tremble as she reread her sister's simple pleas to entreat her mother-in-law to let her visit them that summer, after her exams were over, exams that she would of course never take. He remembers how the day had arrived when she was to take her first Matriculation paper, how he had rushed to tell her that the car had come, watched in horror as she changed her mind while getting into the car about leaving without her mother-in-law's blessing, and wished that he could have held her back as she went indoors in search of her, for he knew then that all was lost. She would never be allowed to sit for the examinations, and more than that, the understanding that had built up between them in these past few months would collapse as she finally surrendered to the circumstances of her new life. And indeed, after this incident she had turned to stone, lay for long periods listlessly upon her bed, hardly wrote letters any more to her family, although they still sent long letters begging her to reply. She never touched her books again, suffered badly in the unfamiliar humidity, and later in the year from the nausea of pregnancy. And he became the gatekeeper of this house, protector of her children, the most faithful and trustworthy of all their servants, who would continue to guard the house and its memories, long after they had all gone.

*

Debendranath Roy eats his supper alone at the great table by the light of a pair of stubby candles, with the gatekeeper's wife fanning him, for the storm has brought down a number of powercables, there is no hope of electricity being restored until tomorrow. He wonders whether the news has reached anybody else that he is alive, that he is in Calcutta, that he may stay here, if it is possible, for the rest of his life. Niharika and the child are at the wedding, he knows that she will tell no one there, in fact he is certain that she will tell no one at all. The decision will be his, when and how to let the world know that he did not drown after all, that for the last twenty years he has successfully hidden himself in a small hillstation in the Himalyas. Of course, the path of least resistance is simply to wait here until the news drifts to them, and they converge upon him, irate, befuddled, but happy that he is alive.

The air is peculiarly still, the candleflame does not waver, as if painted onto the breathless dark, or perhaps it is just that his eyes cannot detect its motion, for his eyes are begining to fail him, deeply fail him. He is glad to be alone in the dark in his first night here, for it is how he sees the days stretching ahead of him, and the dim hurricane lamp in one corner of the drawing room lends it an eerie volume by which he is happy to be diminished. He sits deep into the angle of a long sofa, its arms and back are of canework and carved wood, he enjoys their textures in the darkness, he does not remember them being in this room. And then it strikes him that these are Reba's chairs, the tasteful set that she had purchased for her own rooms, clearly her daughter has found them more acceptable than the plush heavy pieces that sat in this room before, had made the gatekeeper and his minions cart them away and replace them with articles from her mother's room, dragged out all the musical instruments like ailing underventilated children to be left to recover in the sun. This room is but an expanded version of Reba's own chamber, she has finally taken over all of Mandalay.

He walks over to the ghostly assemblage of musical

instruments upon the low platform at the other end of the room, touches them one by one, gently prising off their dustcovers. How could I have forgotten her? he thinks. For no purpose had been served in his life by rising one morning and finding himself released of his obsession with her, it had not freed him to contemplate other relationships, or to fulfil his duties more attentively as a husband and a father, for he was none of these, nor had it given him the peace to pursue with intense dedication some intellectual or artistic goal, for such things had never suffered because of her anyway. And yet, the happiness that he had found was whole without her, gleaned as it was through the pain of loving her, his passion for her had cleansed him, as it never could have if he had not submitted to it so completely, by renouncing everything but his love for her, which he had taken like his only treasure to hide with in the foothills of the Himalayas. How could I have forgotten her? he asks himself now, how could I have forgotten her?

How could he have forgotten her, her long bare arms as she cleaned her instruments, polished them in langorous delight, tuned them to an accuracy that was excruciating to his amateur ear. It had seemed like she was trying to balance each wire on the thin sharp edge of a knife, sometimes it was impossible to bear.

How could he have forgotten her if it were not as the poet said that there was only so much one could forget of love, whereas there was no such limit on love itself, and sitting among the misshapen shadows of her abandoned musical instruments, he realizes what had quietly slipped to one side of his life one morning a few years ago had not ceased to exist, it was just that he had found himself suddenly no longer at the mercy of its ebb and tide, the vast yearning that has consumed him, created him, had deserted him, but he was left in the grace of having once fearlessly succumbed to something stronger than life itself.

The flame of the hurricane lantern at the other end of the room is suddenly extinguished as a great hot wind tears through the swing doors, another storm is following in the wake of the stillness, the monsoon has definitely arrived. He rises from where he kneels among the musical instruments and goes out onto the veranda to meet the first bolt of lightning, the crack of thunder that follows, and then the rain, hard and cold, begins to pelt him from all directions. He feels as if he is crushing himself into a wall of rough rock, in atonement for the sin of deserting them twenty years ago. And if he had not confessed to it today, would it have been a sin, when every sinew of his being had pleaded with him to do it? If he had continued to hide in the hill station for the rest of his days, would he eventually have required some form of repentance of himself?

He returns to his bedchamber soaked to the skin, dries himself in the dark, and puts on some clothes to sleep in, and submits to the awesome savour of her absence that permeates the whole house, even his room which she had hardly ever entered while he occupied it. He feels, as his head sinks into his pillow, as if he has been buried by her side in an ancient crypt, so that finally their flesh might mingle, dragged by maggots from one coffin to the other. Strange that he should think of being buried with her, when they would both doubtless be cremated, and their ashes, unmixed, cast upon the breast of the holy river. But could he bear to be face to face with her again, after this strange long pause? Perhaps it would not be as difficult as he feared, he had after all been loath to behold her when the opportunity had presented itself a few years ago when they were holidaying up the road, he had agonized over whether he could stand to see her in ripe matronage, for she had been but a maiden when he had fallen fruitlessly in love with her, he had been reluctant to set eyes upon her, and yet when he did, he saw that her beauty had not changed, only acquired a certain graveness. Her hair was very grey, and this gave her a more diffuse grace, she looked as if she had been through much pain, and it made him a little wistful to think that it could not be on account of him. No, someone else must have broken her heart, perhaps a string of men, all kept at a perfect distance, but not far enough for her to be insulated from hurt. It seemed to him that he had done far better than her by retreating with her memories to this unlikely haven, but then he had had no other real choice.

He consults the luminous dial of his watch and realizes that it is well past midnight, Niharika and the child have not returned yet from the wedding. He would have liked to hear their voices outside before he fell asleep. He who had blithely abandoned them all twenty years ago, feels a sliver of anxiety that they are not yet back from their unpleasant but hardly perilous journey, but sleep will not wait, sleep has him by the neck now, and is threatening to throttle him if he does not immediately submit to the urge to sink into dreamless oblivion.

He is woken towards dawn by the gatekeeper calling to him from outside the mosquito nets, holding a sooty lantern. What is the matter, demands Debendranath Roy of the old servant, who trembles and replies, the child, sir, she is ill, your niece says we must get a doctor.

Can we telephone Dr Sen? says Debendranath Roy, stepping into his slippers.

Dr Sen died some years ago, says the gatekeeper, I cannot think of how to get a doctor at this time of the night.

But what do you do when you or your wife is ill? he asks.

We go to the hospitals, like other poor people, and wait for hours in stinking queues to be treated. You know how it is, sir. Nothing has changed since you left us. But how can we take her to the filthy hospital, and I do not know where I can find a doctor. I really can't think of what to do.

Can you not go out and scour the streets for some doctor's nameplate – wake him up, it's an emergency.

Sir, I cannot read, sir, your mother tried to teach me once but I never had the patience.

And so it is Debendranath Roy who comes to roam the hot and hungry pavements in the dead of night, squinting through the steam of a dead rainstorm at the faded signs that litter his way, in the hope that one will signal the residence of a doctor, who may be disturbed at this hour without too much pleading, for his tongue is dry in his head, and he would give anything to not have to talk to anyone at any length. Even as he searches, tripping over ends of rough pavement and into fresh puddles, even as he searches, he cannot help but muse upon the image of his mother trying to teach the young gatekeeper his letters. It would have been in her home in North Bengal, he surmises, there rather than within the starched halls of Mandalay, there upon the long veranda, he can see a reed mat scattered with books, and his mother gently giggling as the gatekeeper, then simply a servant's young son, tries vainly to copy out his name.

It proves to be reasonably easy to find a doctor, a young man who hurriedly throws on his clothes, and walks back with him in sleepy silence to Mandalay, where the child is lying upon the vast bed, moaning softly. The gatekeeper's wife tries to cool her with a broken bamboo fan, and Niharika stands beside holding a vomit pail.

Damned power cuts, exclaims the doctor, groping in his case. Hold the lantern high, he commands the gatekeeper.

I think it is just something she ate, says the doctor, eventually. But I will take a blood sample anyway, there is a lot of malaria around these days.

By the time he is finished, the sun is rising. They ask him if he would like to join them for a cup of tea.

They sit down at the dining table, the gatekeeper's wife brings them three steaming cups of sweet milky brew. What a marvellous table, says the doctor, running his hands over its pitted mahogany surface, just starting to become visible in the morning light.

If any of the furniture here interests you, says Debendranath Roy, please let us know, we might be able to negotiate a price.

Niharika stares at him, aghast.

Not much of it would fit in our flat, laughs the young doctor, but perhaps some of the smaller things . . .

When he has gone, Debendranath Roy apologizes. I can see

that you are shocked, he says, but I desperately need the money.

What makes you think it is yours to sell? she asks.

Some of it should be, he says confidently.

How did you get by anyway? she asks suddenly. How did you manage to keep body and soul together in the hill station?

I actually had a little bank account that I had kept secret from your aunt – she was so neurotic about money, although she never begrudged me any of my vices, god bless her, poor soul. I managed to take the money out of it and close it on the afternoon of my 'death'. It was enough to set me up in this small hill town. I found a cheap room to rent, and ate very frugally, until I found that I could make a reasonable living mending china for the wives of the teaplanters.

Mending china?

Yes, it was a strange accident really. To give my little room some colour, I had planted a few odd herbs and things in earthenware pots – mainly of the kind they use to sell yoghurt, for then I could purchase my plantpot and dinner with the same rupee. One evening I came home to find that a rabbit that I was keeping for company had upset and broken one of the pots, in an effort to eat the plant.

Did you banish the rabbit?

No, on the contrary, it lived a good ten years, and gave me much joy. But, to return to the plantpot . . . for some reason, I was heartbroken that such a thing should have happened, and once I had swept the dirt from the floor, I sat there with the broken pieces in my hand, slowly turning them between my fingers, and finally fitting them together into a whole, which the following morning I consolidated with a precious tube of glue. I had never felt more fulfilled in my life.

And so you found your metier?

No need to be sarcastic. I told the story to a retired surgeon whom I would sometimes accompany on his morning walk, and that afternoon he came to me with a favourite meer-schaum pipe, which had been split into two by a grandchild some years before. If you can fix this, he told me, I will pay you anything. It was harder with something that had got used to being broken, whose edges were no longer newly jagged, but I worked at it with a concentration so fierce that I hardly knew how the pieces flew about among my fingers and coalesced almost magically into the whole. After that, I was never short of work, and soon I was able to rent a small house, which is where I lived all these years, says Debendranath Roy.

Have you been happy there? she asks.

Very happy, he replies.

Then why are you here? she asks. What has made you emerge after all these years from your splendid seclusion?

I am going blind, he tells her. I was told, a few months ago, that I was sure to lose my sight within the next few years. That night, I dreamt I was in Mandalay again, as I often did, but this time I could not see, and yet it did not seem to matter, for I still knew where everything was, could still smell each hour of the day, feel the dusk deepen into night, and then I knew that I had to come back, that life would be bearable, even in blindness, within the walls of Mandalay.

She is silent for a long time. Finally she says, that was not what I was expecting at all.

What were you expecting? he asks.

I don't know, she says. But I have spent the last two years trying to reinvent you, and now you are here, I hardly know where my character ends and you begin, perhaps it is simply not within the logic of my book for you to go blind, I do not know.

In your book – surely I am dead? he asks.

Yes, indeed, but your death has a thousand shapes, she answers.

And none of these are where I do not die at all, but go blind in my fifties, and return to live alone among the ruins of this house?

Why do you think you will have to live alone? asks his niece. I'm sure Jennifer will be willing to take care of you.

I wouldn't want that.

That would be cruel. It is what she has been waiting for all her life.

But it would be so unfair, that I should desert her in the prime of my health, and then ask her to tend to me in my blindness. No, it would choke me, he says.

Even though it may be the best thing for both of you?

Even so, says Debendranath Roy.

By lunchtime the child has recovered from the episode of fever and vomiting of the previous night, but is still too weak to join them at the table. He has sat with her for most of the morning, chatting and playing cardgames. She is easy to amuse, and her smiles fill him with such good cheer that he cannot help wondering whether he should have persevered within the circumstances that he had created for himself twenty years ago, become an academic, had children with Jennifer, filled his back garden with Wendy Houses and paddling pools, taken them to museums and to the movies, it could have worked after a fashion. But looking deep within him, he cannot see any real regret that he had abandoned that life, except that he had drawn a line at the same time through the lives of others, of Jennifer especially, whom he had loved.

Did you ever come across Nicholas Faraday? he asks his niece at lunch.

Oh, I saw a lot of them, she says. They were very kind to Jennifer when she moved to Oxford, and we visited them regularly. I would see Rosemary sometimes on her own when she came into town. They are very dear to me, she said.

And their son? he asked. Daniel, how is he?

I have not seen him since they moved to Australia, about five years ago.

What did he end up doing with his life?

He is a very successful photographer I believe.

Did he marry? Does he have any children?

Yes, he is married, and he has a son.

He was a wonderful boy, says Debendranath Roy, with much affection. I used to play chess with him when I visited them. He was just a schoolboy then. Sometimes we would go for walks through the countryside. It was a difficult time for me, and being in his company gave me more hope than almost anything else.

He believes that he was the last person to have seen you alive.

That he was, for a while at least.

But not anymore, she says.

Do you not have the urge, he asks her, do you not feel like telling him so?

No, she replies truthfully, for it pales in comparison with the five years worth of things to tell him that she has trapped within her.

Do you not feel like telling anyone that I have surfaced from the dead? he asks.

I need to absorb it myself first, she says.

I could always just disappear in the night and leave you wondering whether I was simply a complex delusion.

She shakes her head. The girl, she says, the girl would speak of you, and that would make you real, even though nothing else might, not the gatekeeper's protestations that he had hauled bathwater up two flights of stairs for you, or his wife's insistence that you had happily eaten the meals she had cooked for you. But if the child remembered you, it would be hard to deny.

Hard to deny to the rest of the family?

I was thinking more of myself. They will not believe it anyway. My sister-in-law is bound to think it was an impersonator, she has a suspicious mind.

And you? he asks. Do you believe this is really me?

I have been used to living with you as a figment of my imagination, she says. It does not make that much difference to me whether you are real or not.

He is silent for a while. What are you thinking? she asks.

I am thinking who could have taken away the softness in you, he replies. What is it that you have learnt to live with that has given you a surface of slate?

What was it that you could not learn to live with, she retorts, what was it that you could not bear to live with that you decided to fake your own death?

If it is the same thing then I strongly recommend my course of action, he says.

I thought that was exactly what I was doing, without taking the trouble to fool the world in the meantime that I was dead.

Then perhaps it is just that you have long to wait, says Debendranath Roy.

That I do not doubt, she says. For two years of waiting in silence had done nothing to soothe the ache within her. She still woke dreaming that Daniel was sitting at the foot of her bed, or waiting quietly in the drawing room, smoking a thin cigar, and trying to guess the shapes of the musical instruments in their faded shrouds. He would have made a detour on one of his missions to Asia, I had to see you, he would tell her, I had to see you. Every morning she searched through the mail with the painful anticipation she had not felt since she was a child, and sometimes she would find herself wandering out onto the veranda with her afternoon tea to wait for the postman, even though by then any dreamfed presentiment would have withered. But the sight of the postman still brought a surge of hope which she could not help but treasure, for it was all she had.

She hoped too for some word from Morgan, but it was as if a mile of fog had risen between them that it would be obscene to try and navigate. She had written letters to him but thrown each one away, crushing them into the waste paper basket with vehemence lest they should threaten to resurrect themselves. The ball was neither in his court nor hers, it seemed unlikely that communication would ever be re-established. She thought of him often, and strangely it was the image of him after a snowball fight that came to her most often. Despite his resolve never to visit Princeton again, he had come down occasionally to see her, almost always unannounced, and this time he had surprised her outside the building as she was emerging from a painting course she had decided to take as a diversion from her work. How did you know I would be here, she asked. You told me so when we spoke on the phone two hours ago, he said, you told me you were on your way to your art class, where else could you be but here? And then he had flung at her the ball of snow that he had been shaping in his gloved hands while he was waiting for her to emerge. She had been surprised at this gesture, for it seemed shockingly physical for someone like Morgan who seemed to have eschewed that part of his being a long time ago, who lived so deeply in a land of ideas that even food was only acceptable to him as an exultantly pure concept – a single delectable oyster, a morsel of supremely fresh tuna tinged slightly with the paste of green horseradish on its small firm bed of perfect ricegrains. But the only way to respond with kindness was to fling some snow at him. She had hardly time to pack it into a decent ball before the rhythm of the game dissolved, and the embarrassment of this unlikely act came to overwhelm them. And then some form of snowfight had issued, and continued long enough to justify and absolve, even obliterate that ponderous moment when his snowball had hit her face and she had wondered, why, why? And yet, now when she remembers him, it is with his long black overcoat swinging wide as his long thin arm flew in a circle to aim his powdery missile, snow in his black hair and on his narrow shoulders, it had been a snowfight without laughter, only smiles, as if they were practising for a serious match or a secret mission, for he and she were partners somehow, partners already in sleuthing the pygmy, partners in the crime of loving Daniel Faraday, partners in loathing anything but the truth, however stark, however painful. And as they fought in the snow, their battle had become a rite of passage into this stern tryst, where they would be true to each other as lovers cannot possibly ever be, here was an alliance of complete honesty, and it was true that she had never lied to him, could never think of lying to him, and yet now, the space that he occupied is empty, she fears he will never come back.

Ochre

That afternoon, at the pharmacy around the corner she encounters the doctor who had come to see her niece in the early hours of the day. He does not look as youthful in the light. He is filling his case with medicines, how is the child? he asks.

She seems to have recovered, but she looks very weak.

Make sure she takes lots of fluids, he says almost automatically, as he counts tablets.

Where are you taking these? she asks.

He tells her that he works for three days a week in a village clinic, that he has done so for almost ten years now. It is a very different experience, he says.

They walk back together in the direction of their homes. I did not realize that there was anybody living in your house, he says to her as they reach the gates of Mandalay.

I have been rather reclusive, she admits.

Well, everyone else seemed to know that you were here, it is just that I am hardly ever at home, and when I am I hardly pay any attention to what anyone is saying.

He gazes through the rusty gates towards the decaying mansion. As children, we used to wonder what your lives were like behind these high walls, he says. We saw you sometimes, and your twin brothers, and the cousins and friends that surrounded you, and we used to try and imagine what you did together in such a large house, how you would ever find each other if you played hide-and-seek. We used to think how lucky you were that if you wanted chocolate bars or cakes from Flury's all you needed to do was tell the driver, we used to envy you the new toys we sometimes caught a glimpse of, the shiny red scooter that your brothers rode in circles on the driveway, in and out of the portico, we watched them sometimes, and when they played cricket it was always with a proper deuce ball and pads. We were in awe of you, and yet sometimes, for no apparent reason, we felt sad for you, we never knew why, except that our elders spoke of a curse on the family, of an uncle drowning, but that was not why our hearts were sometimes filled with a tender sorrow for you.

We used to see your mother, he says, as she was driven to her rehearsals, her beauty left us speechless. We went to her concerts sometimes, and to her plays. She was a most wonderful actress, your mother. The only other time I have been in your house was when I played a small part in a play which she allowed us to rehearse there once, even though she had decided not to act in it, this was shortly before they left for Delhi. You had already gone.

Is that how you spend the rest of your time then? she asks. In the theatre?

We are doing 'The Threepenny Opera' tomorrow, he says. I will send you some tickets if you say you will come. It is a Bengali translation, of course.

But not adapted to nineteenth century Calcutta?

No, we will be dressed as English beggars.

I should love to come, she replies.

Very well then, I will arrange for some tickets to be sent to you. Bring the girl, he says, I believe in exposing children to serious art at an early age.

Do you think she will be well enough?

I should think so.

You *are* her doctor.

And the gentleman who woke me up this morning, should I send a ticket for him?

I do not know whether he will come, although I have heard that he did have a taste for such things once.

Is he a relative?

He is my uncle, she replies. He is the uncle who was supposed to have drowned twenty years ago.

I thought it was all a rumour, says the doctor.

Oh, the shark has pretty teeth dear, and he shows them a pearly white, just a jack-knife has MacHeath dear, and he keeps it out of sight.

She remembers her mother upon the stage as she had seen her last, in the role of Medea, which she played with such reserve that Niharika was nervous that for once she had been totally miscast as the embittered foreign sorceress deserted by her ambitious husband. But when the time came to slit the throats of her children, she felt the audience throbbing with her grief, and herself almost nauseated by the calmness with which she took their lives, the movements of a woman stunned beyond reason by the failure of love, for it had seemed to her then that it resonated too closely with the grand vein of unhappiness that ran through her mother's life. Not the anxiety of being discarded by her husband, never that of course, but the price she had paid to insure herself against that, and perhaps generally against the vagaries of a man's heart.

I wish you had not come, her mother said to her in the green room, as she was changing. It felt awful to be playing the role of woman who kills her children with you in the audience.

But my brothers have been to see the play as well, she said.

That did not matter so much, said Reba. Perhaps because they are men now, with their own lives, I love them dearly as my sons, but there is a distance there. That distance is not there with you. And now, you are about to go off and make a life of your own, but I suspect I will always feel attached to you like this, perhaps it is because you are the only one I suckled, the twins were impossible to breastfeed and I was so unwell after their birth. But you fed at my breast until you were almost a year old, said her mother as she took off her stage make-up, perhaps it was only to you that I really gave a piece of myself.

When the shark bites with his teeth dear, scarlet billows start to spread, fancy gloves though wears MacHeath dear, so there's not a trace of red.

You have my heart, but not my affiliation, Daniel Faraday had told her, stroking her cheek, just after he had made love to her, you know that you have my heart, but my allegiances lie elsewhere, dear, I hope you can live with that, dear, it is a better thing to live with than many other things I can think of, dear.

Like sharing a cage in the zoo with an orang utan, for instance?

Far better even than that, dear, he had said to her, kissing her several times on the top of her head. We each find our way, dear, to live a life without too many lies – this is mine, dear – you still have to figure out what is yours.

And briefly she was filled with hope, here was a puzzle he was setting out for her, perhaps once she had solved it, he would find it easier to come back to her, meanwhile he would pick his mistresses so that they did not poach upon his life.

On the sidewalk Sunday morning lies a body oozing life, someone's sneaking round the corner, can that someone be Mack the Knife?

After the performance, which is in a small intimate theatre on the top floor of the German cultural centre, the doctor leaps off the stage to greet her without bothering to change his costume. I am so glad you came, he says to her, although at one point I thought I myself might not make it, the train was held up for almost an hour because there was a dead buffalo on the tracks. I only just got here in time.

She is amazed at his energy, he must have woken at some very early hour to get to his village surgery, spent the day seeing patients, and then rushed straight here to play MacHeath, which he did with much wicked verve. You are quite remarkable, she tells him.

And did you like the play? he asks her niece.

It's the best play I have ever seen, she says truthfully, for it is her first experience of theatre outside school pantomimes.

Have you eaten, he asks, shall we go for Chinese food?

You must be exhausted, she says. But the child is already hopping up and down at the thought of going to a restaurant with this extraordinary man.

Don't worry, he says, I am used to it. Give me a few minutes to change my clothes. In the restaurant the child mistakes a bottle of chilli sauce for tomato ketchup and screams in agony at her first mouthful of chicken chow mein. Don't worry, he tells her, drink lots of water, and have some plain rice, the pain will soon go away.

She has learnt from the playbill that his name is Rahul Mitra, and she is suddenly deeply curious about the rest of his life. As they talk, a picture slowly forms of a relentness pattern of activity that has left no time for much else. He has lived all his life just down the road from them, in a second floor flat in a reasonably elegant old house, went to a missionary school within walking distance of them, and then to a medical college, trained in Delhi for a few years, but returned to Calcutta without furthering his career, to divide his time between his father's fairly prosperous practice and the village clinic. It pleased her that there seemed to be no anguished violence in his commitment to tend to the poor, it is a very interesting job, he told her, there is always something to surprise me there, whereas here it is just the run of the mill heart complaint or asthma or some little girl who has eaten too many sweets and feels very sick in the middle of the night, he says teasingly to her niece, ruffling her hair.

I didn't eat too may sweets at the wedding! the girl protests.

And sometimes, he says, at the village clinic, a boy will come in with some minor ailment but you will see by the light in his eyes that it is not that he really wishes to consult you about, but some route out of the situation he has been born into. He wants to study, go to university, find out what it is that makes the earth go round the sun, and not the other way. Perhaps that is the most rewarding part for me.

What do you do for them? she asks.

Often I induct them into our theatre group, it is a good way of opening their eyes. Sometimes, they make something out of it, more often they are sidetracked by the city lights, but some have worked their way into what we think of as respectable professions, which is of course just another level of misery, urban rather than rural, but at least they will have gained something in studying to be a petty clerk or a technician.

And are there never any girls?

They do not come to me.

Who do they go to, then? she asks.

I really do not know, he says.

Do you not think that is unfair?

It does not concern me, he says. I am there to cure people of their gout and intestinal worms, whatever else happens along the way is just a bonus, that is all.

Would you take me with you on one of your visits? she asks.

With pleasure, he says. As long as you do not write a novel about it, he adds smiling.

You do not like my style of writing? she asks.

I haven't had the time to read any of your books, he confesses. But I was only joking, we are very proud of you in the neighbourhood, and I would be honoured if you accompanied me to my village clinic, but I warn you it could all be rather dull.

It would have to be soon, she says, I leave for England in two weeks.

I am going on Friday, if you would like to come, he says.

That would suit me very well, she says.

They walk back through the hot night to their neighbourhood and when they reach Mandalay, they find that the gates are flung open as if in the wake of some disaster, the driveway is full of cars, someone must have finally got wind of Debendranath Roy's reappearance, the family have arrived.

*

Why did you not tell us? the elder of her twin brothers asks. The other twin is still in the United States, and their father is too ill to travel, he and her mother are conspicuously absent from the confused and tearful crowd of aunts and cousins. Debendranath Roy has locked himself in his room, he does not wish to see anyone, the gatekeeper tells them.

You have virtually been sheltering a criminal, her brother tells her.

And what was his crime?

The man pretended to have died, for God's sake.

It's not as if he ran off with his own life insurance. It was a sin perhaps, but not a crime.

Well that is worse then, is it not?

Surely that depends on the quality of the sin.

Well, I can think of no worse sin, says her brother.

At least it is a sin of colour, she says, at least it is a sin of colour, a sin of proper beauty and not some mean thing.

What? says her brother.

Just a line from one of my favourite plays, she replies.

This is not a time for poetry, he says.

She finds her uncle standing at the window, gazing out at the cemetery where she had walked with him as a child. What will you do now? she asks.

Will they not eventually disperse? he asks. How long can they hold me under siege?

I do not know, she says, sitting down on the bed.

It is better in the winter when it is foggy.

The view of the cemetery?

Yes.

I have walked there in the winter just after sunrise, it is pleasant to be among the gravestones in the morning mist.

That is how I envisaged my blindness, says Debendranath Roy.

I think you should agree to talk to my brother, she says. It will not be pleasant, but I feel it is necessary, he is crude, but also compassionate.

And so a message is sent through the gatekeeper to invite him to join them, the elder of the twins, always his favourite of the two, now oozing the unripe confidence of a man in his early thirties for whom things have been going well but not for long enough for him to be certain that they will go well forever, he struts in and orders his sister to leave. This is between men, he attempts to convince them.

I don't see how that can be, says their uncle. I want her to stay.

We have to negotiate your position in this family after twenty years of pretending to be dead, says his nephew, it may not be so pleasant.

What exactly do we need to determine? asks Debendranath Roy.

Whether you have relinquished your claim on your birthright and your share of the family fortune by having declared yourself dead.

It was not I who declared myself dead, he says.

Let us not use detail as a diversion from the more serious points.

But if I had gone out to buy cigarettes and never returned, would you have assumed that I was dead? It just so happened that I was lying in a boat when I made the decision not to go back home.

If we had had no word from you in twenty years, I think we would have assumed you were dead no matter what, says his nephew. But that is hardly the point, he adds, the real question is what you want to do now, what you want us to do now, now that you have come back from the dead.

I came back, says Debendranath Roy, because I am going blind. So, I suppose you could say that I seek shelter, for the money that I have will not last too long, and certainly not for the many years that I may live yet.

His nephew's eyes soften, are you certain, he asks shakily, that you are going blind?

I would like not to be certain, he says.

His nephew sits down upon the bed and starts to sob quietly with his head against the carved bedpost. So you did not come back because of us, he says.

I have returned in the worst hour of my need, he says, but that does not mean I have not come back because of you.

How so?

One is a need, the other a want, says Debendranath Roy, but one does not diminish the other, no more than the necessity of food can dull the desire for music, I have said enough, now please let me be.

His nephew paces the length of the room a few times without speaking, then he says: you must understand that it is not just a matter of your being alive, by re-entering our lives you have become our responsibility, we will take care of you, but you must tell us how.

Very well, then. All I want to do is live here, in Mandalay, and I suppose I must be fed and clothed. I have money enough for that for a while, but when it runs out, I shall be at your mercy.

We still have a few interests in Calcutta, says his nephew, which we could ask you to oversee, while you still have your sight, and then pay you a pension when it becomes necessary.

That would not suit me at all, says Debendranath Roy.

I am trying to help, says his nephew.

I appreciate that, he replies, but you must understand that for twenty years now I have lived like a hermit, sealed myself away in the hills with people who are but relics of the Raj, retired teaplanters, old army colonels. I have spent twenty years mending their absurd china, their Attic Wedgewood, their Waterford crystal, which they value almost above their lives, which is why I have been able to live in comfort and peace. But to descend from that into supervising your petty little bicycle pump and baby bottle companies would be a fate worse than death for me, I am afraid to say.

You do not mince your words, do you? says his nephew.

If you can just let me stay here, and make sure that I am if, and there is someone to help me up the stairs to my room, I will be very grateful, says Debendranath Roy.

Again his nephew paces the room, he does not say anything, only sometimes he draws his breath as if he were trying to stifle a sob.

We will do that for you, he says finally. We will make sure that you are clothed and fed while you live, and we will leave you alone, we will not visit you or write to you unless it is truly pressing, we will ignore you, like this house, like our past.

That would suit me very well, his uncle replies.

And now I will leave, and you will forgive me if I do not touch your feet in the usual gesture of respect, for respect is the one thing I cannot offer you, says his nephew.

I would never ask it, says Debendranath Roy.

I will leave now, says his nephew. I have a room booked in the hotel where I usually stay when I come here on business, and tomorrow I will take the morning flight back to Delhi. I am going to take my daughter with me now, I do not feel comfortable about her being in this house.

I would like to say goodbye to her.

She is asleep, says Niharika. I told her to go to bed, and she obeyed without any hesitation, she has had an exciting day.

Wake her up then, says her father. I do not intend to leave without her. And so the child is dragged out of bed, dressed and taken to say goodbye to Debendranath Roy, she clings in sleepy confusion to Niharika. What about the trip to the village with Rahul? she asks. How can I go with you if I leave for Delhi tomorrow?

We can save that for your next visit, she soothes her.

But you are leaving soon, the girl says sullenly.

I will come back, promises Niharika. And meanwhile you must write to me whenever you can, and tell me everything that happens to you, and everything that you want to happen to you, so that perhaps I can make it happen, if that is possible.

Say goodbye to Rahul for me, says the girl as she climbs into the car with her father.

I will, replies Niharika.

And indeed it is the first question he asks her on Friday morning, when she meets him alone at the train station. Where is your niece? She is not ill again, I hope, he says as she approaches him by the ticket counter. He has already been to see a few patients in the slums near the railway station, and is wonderfully alert, while she is still struggling to wake up properly. She has grown accustomed to working late into the night, and sleeping until lunchtime. His timetable does not suit her at all.

It takes just over an hour to reach the village. The train is crowded with peasants returning from the market. They must have woken before dawn to make the journey with their vegetables and broiler chickens, now they return to tend their small plots, feed their animals and their families. A woman with a baby approaches Rahul Mitra. She has identified him as one of the clinic doctors. He keeps sucking, she says desperately, but nothing comes.

Take this when you get home and try and sleep a little in the afternoon, he says to her, handing her a small plastic bottle.

It's only some brandy and sugar water, he tells Niharika in English.

Does it work?

I don't know, he replies. It helps to take something that a doctor has given them.

But won't the alcohol get into the breastmilk?

There is very little alcohol, he says. It does not do them any harm. It will be much worse if she really cannot breastfeed and they have to give it diluted cow's milk, or worse still if they start giving it watered down formula milk.

Poor girl, she says, watching her trying to comfort her wailing child.

She works the dawn shift in a factory, he tells her.

He wipes the perspiration from his forehead with an unnaturally white handkerchief. He winces a little as a stiff corner pokes him in his eye. I wish my mother would not starch these, he says.

They finally disembark at a small station surrounded by paddy fields. The sky is white from the fury of the sun. I usually walk, he says, but we can take a cycle rickshaw if you prefer.

I would rather walk, she says. She does not wish to share a narrow seat with him, to be jostled together upon the rough dirt road, that would not be the way she would first like him to touch her, to have their wet wrists clash as the rickshaw swerved to avoid a pothole, or for her coil of hair to come loose as they go over a treacherous bump and fall like dead grass into his hands.

She takes a small folding umbrella from her bag and opens it to shield her from the sun, and then they walk together through the rice fields to the village. I love this walk, he tells her, I love it best on winter mornings, when the air is crisp, and the sun is not an enemy, and it is a vast relief to leave the city smog behind. But even in this heat, I look forward to this stretch of sweet silence. I have been addicted to rural Bengal ever since I was a boy. You see, my father worked for a few years in a remote part of Medinipur when we were quite young. We stayed in Calcutta with our grandparents, and visited them during our vacations. He was posted to an area where there were no suitable schools, and hardly any other people, and my brothers and I would amuse ourselves by playing in the fields all day, it was bliss.

I hardly know rural Bengal, she says quietly.

When I was young, you could still get a sense of it in the southern fringes of the city where many of my relatives lived. I loved to visit them there, and go chasing mongrel dogs and scabby chickens by the ponds, but now these areas have been swallowed by the city, and are crowded with multistoried apartment blocks. It was inevitable, I suppose, says Rahul.

They reach the clinic and he puts on his white coat which hangs beside the door upon a large nail. She likes how he looks in it, and smiles as he stands aside and shows her the way in to the room where he receives patients. A man has just finished washing the cement floor, and it smells strongly of disinfectant, which fills her with a mild and slightly unfocussed pleasure which she interprets as the beginnings of desire.

The first few patients come in with the usual run of complaints, and he deals with them easily, annotating each case lightly for her benefit. But then a leper enters, and despite herself, she cannot bear to look upon the horribly burnt hands that he holds out to Rahul, who tends to them, and explains that it is not the disease itself that causes so much disfigurement as the lack of sensation whereby a man will plunge his hands into boiling water or hold a hot coal between his fingers without feeling the harm that is done. The next is a woman with a terrible eye disease, and Niharika begins to feel that she cannot take much more. She tells him so, and he smiles and nods and suggests that she goes for a walk around the village. He would be another hour or so, for there were not many patients today, and morning clinics were always less oversubscribed than the afternoon sessions, for it was a time when most of these people had to work, whether they felt ill or not, he explains. It pleases her that there is never a trace of bitterness in him when he states these cruel facts, nor does he seem to gain any satisfaction from speculating on who is to blame for all this, although she is certain that he holds strong opinions on the subject, opinions that he does not wish to devalue by voicing in support of his dedication to his work, opinions that he does not wish to squander upon the impatient and the uneducated, and certainly not upon her.

She leaves the clinic and makes her way towards a plain brick structure she sees in the distance which she surmises is a school. And as she comes close, she hears the familiar drone within it of children trying to learn by rote what they feel least inclined to know. And yet among these, there will be a young mind to whom the names of the rivers of Bengal are magic, like coloured streamers upon the tongue, as they had been to her grandmother, Neerupama, many years ago in a small school in an insignificant town in North Bengal, when the world had suddenly arrayed itself like lozenges upon the pages of her geography book, the five continents, each with its countries and rivers and forests, its own great mountains, its own proud deserts, its own history of calamities.

The gatekeeper sits upon his haunches, trying to clean the inside of his old transistor radio in the hope that it might work again. Miraculously, as he tightens the last screw, it jerks back into life, issuing a series of faint crackles, like blood from a stone, and he remembers how this was often the best they could get, seventy years ago, in the small town in North Bengal. He had never dreamt in the wildest of his dreams that he would possess a radio someday, and that it would be small enough for him to hold in one hand. One of the twin boys had given it to him when they had left home. It was old now, and clogged easily with dust. In the doctor's house in North Bengal, the radio had been one of their most precious possessions, in its great wooden case and its many dials. He would always watch from a distance as they fiddled with it in holy frustration until finally the signal came through, the news bulletins and the latest cricket match scores, and the children would dance with glee, all of them except Neerupama, who would sit entranced by the commentator's voice. It made her head reel to think that it came from so far away, she would try and imagine where he was, what he saw while he spoke for all of Bengal to hear. She envied the great responsibility on his shoulders. He was like a man upon the mast who is trying to describe the land that he sees ahead to the others on the deck.

She spoke often of distant lands, and once she had roped him into a game that no one else would play with her, where they pretended to travel around the coast of Africa, here is the Pepper Coast, she said, and now we are coming to the Ivory Coast . . .

He knew that she spent a lot of her time poring over a

motheaten atlas or scribbling in an exercise book about foreign lands. The headmaster of the village school would lend her books written explorers which he saw her devour by the light of hurricane lamps sitting on a mat upon the veranda, until her mother came and took them away, said that she would ruin her eyes if she read any more.

She pulled him by his arm, be careful, she said, for we are entering the Gold Coast . . .

Where is Africa? he had asked.

Very far away, she had answered with a dismissive toss of her head. Here now is the Slave Coast, she said, where they will catch you and put you on board a ship to America and there you will live without your freedom, as the possession of a family, you will never be able to run away.

Niharika wanders upon the network of narrow paths between the paddy fields and the low ponds overgrown with water hyacinths. Children pass her and are sometimes arrested by her urban appearance, her stiff white sari only faintly touched with mud, her different bearing, her unfamiliar gait, the little green umbrella that she holds. She had bought it on her last trip to New York from one of those shops that prides itself on kitting you out for tropical adventures, it claimed to be unusually compact and hardwearing, it had never suspected while it was on its assembly line in New Jersey or wherever, that it would actually find itself in a village in Bengal. Even in its simple sturdiness it is incongruous among the tall palms and the fetid mudpools. She sees, ahead of her, the shell of an old feudal home, in vermilion brick, with its crenellated parapets still held proudly against the sky, its tall windows hung with toothless shutters, and as she walks through the opening that was once its front door, she is overcome by the feeling that this will be the future of Mandalay, that one day she will come up the portico stairs and find that all that remains of the grand drawing room are its four long walls, still hung with their family portraits, thick with dust.

Standing among the ruins of this nameless house, she dreams that she has come back after many years to her childhood home to find it in a state of sublime decay, overrun with thick green creepers, birds' nests crowding its roofless stairwells, a row of lanterns swinging blindly from the last remaining beam in the kitchen. And in his room overlooking the cemetery her uncle will still be sitting in his old armchair, holding in his hands the books he once so loved but can now no longer read, he will be sitting in the murk of his own vision as she had once imagined him to perch upon a throne of coral in an underwater kingdom, peering through the salty gloom at the mermaid who had led him there, a sweet mermaid who had found him injured by the river where they said he had drowned.

She sees him stand up and stretch, in the distant future, and grope around for the small bell he uses to summon the gatekeeper, she sees him ask for him to play a record upon the old gramophone that he now keeps in his room, not that one you idiot, she hears him say to the old servant. But sir, you know I cannot read, pleads the gatekeeper. Let me describe the cover to you again, says Debendranath Roy. It has the face of a woman. He tries to describe her, and then realizes it is futile, for so many of them have a photograph of the artiste on the cover. Bring them to me, he commands the gatekeeper, in the hope that he might be able to distinguish them by touch. All of them? asks the gatekeeper. All of them, he says. But there are so many, protests the gatekeeper. Then just bring me a few, he says. And Niharika covers her face as she sees the gatekeeper stumble with a pile of records and send them crashing onto the pitted marble floor, she cannot bear to continue with this vision, she moves further into the depths of the ruins, and tries to imagine life as it was for the family that once lived here, and banish all thoughts of the future of her own kin.

So much of the interior has simply vanished behind the grand facade, she can hardly make out where the rooms might have been, the parlours and the music rooms, the inner sanctum where the women had lived out their priveleged lives, while the men conducted their business in the outer regions of the house. What has happened to their descendants, she wonders, has the family died out, or are they spread about the city, slaving in humid offices, ferrying their offspring back and forth to school, haggling over the price of aubergines at the local market with the grandsons of the very peasants who had once been in their thrall? Perhaps they were Mussalmans who had been frightened by Parition into moving eastwards, abandoning their lands, just as her family had moved westwards, quitting forever their ancestral home in the region of rivers, now part of a different country, where Debendranath Roy had been born during the war. They had been evacuated there from Calcutta, and her father had told her many stories of their life in the village, how he and his cousins would frolic among the fisherfolk, ride on their elephant, tease the monkeys, befriend the stray dogs, frighten their mothers by shimmying up tall trees to pick the fruit. She remembered that he had spoken often of these days to his younger brother in the year that they lived in Calcutta, but Debendranath Roy had always replied that he had been too young to remember much of that magical land of rivers where he had learnt to punt a boat across a flooded plain almost before he could properly walk. Who knows what happened to our house? her father would say, and her uncle would shrug as if he did not really want to be unified with his brother in nostalgia, an attitude that she was somehow able to perceive even as a child, and which made her run away from them to a part of the house where she could not hear them at all.

She turns around as she hears footsteps, it is Rahul. I thought I would find you here, he says. Come away, it is dangerous, a whole section might collapse upon you any minute.

I am sorry, she says, picking her way out of the rubble. I was so mesmerized by its beauty that it did not even occur to me that it might be unstable, she apologizes.

Were you thinking of how such a fate might befall your own

home? he asks, holding his hand out for her to grip as she climbs over the last few bricks.

That was the essence of the morbid attraction, I suppose.

Well, let me assure you then that much worse awaits it, for I am certain that as soon as they are able to win your father's permission, your brothers will raze it to the ground and build blocks of luxury apartments on the prime site that it occupies.

They have promised my uncle they will let him live there, she says.

I should not think that he will have much say in the matter, especially if he is going blind.

Niharika sighs as she recalls her vision of Debendranath Roy in the great house alone, his eyesight failing a little more every day, she cannot bear to think of him as defenceless, I feel responsible for him, she tells Rahul.

Even though he blithely left you all in the shadow of his death, so that he might have the prime of his life all to himself, and now has returned because he is no longer able to take care of himself on his own?

Even so.

I am glad you say that, says Rahul.

The gatekeeper looks up to find Debendranath Roy walking down the driveway dressed as if he might be going out, and carrying a long umbrella. He has not left the premises since he arrived five days ago. I thought I would go for a stroll, he says.

If you need the car, it is here, says the gatekeeper. The driver has been idle since he returned from dropping Niharika at the railway station, and the gatekeeper does not like this. He feels he should be occupied, even though there is no one to take anywhere, and no errands to run in this household of ghosts and old maids.

I am just going for a short walk, says Debendranath Roy, steering past him into the street. But as soon as he is outside the gates of Mandalay his legs feel weak, his eyes seem unable to focus in the blinding sunlight. Nonetheless, he grips his umbrella and begins to walk down the street, taking note of the many changes that have occurred in the last twenty years, that had not made so much of an impression on him when he had approached his childhood home five days ago to declare himself returned from the dead. The roads and pavements are actually in somewhat better condition than in 1975, he decides, but what little was left then of the grace of the city has now completely disappeared. He watches a gaggle of school-girls emerging from a plastic faced ice-cream parlour licking their dripping cones and chattering in a horrible sounding English. How could we have come to this? he wonders, how could we have come to this?

He walks a little further and comes upon the little shop where he used to buy cigarettes as a student, he is thankful that it is still there, just a little hole really in the wall of a small block of old flats, still stocked with cheap toffees and *paan* spices, and bottled colas and lemonades in a coolbox stuffed with dirty ice. He asks for a soft drink, and the man looks at him strangely as he hands him the bottle. Can it be that he recognizes him as an old customer, the younger of Indranath Roy's sons, said to have drowned many years ago. And then he realizes that the whole neighbourhood must know by now that he has returned to Mandalay, that he had not drowned at all, simply lived in secret in the Himalayas for twenty years. Perhaps they think he is a criminal of some sort, that he had been on the run from the law, or from some other menace which had recently passed, and allowed him to emerge from his hiding place. He tips the bottle up to drink and finds himself looking up at a woman who quickly pulls a curtain across the window from where she has been watching him. He feels a strong nausea as he looks around to another balcony where a young boy is unabashedly staring in his direction, he can hear his mother urging him to stop and come inside, it is clear that they all know who he is, that they are all watching him.

He returns the empty bottle to the shopkeeper and pays for

the soft drink, and then he turns and with his eyes fixed upon the ground he walks straight back to Mandalay. He has become a prisoner within its walls already, he realizes. Perhaps he will be able to walk outside again when he is blind, when he cannot see the faces of his neighbours, and read upon them their gruesome speculations as to the nature of his disappearance and the reasons for his return. He goes indoors and washes the perspiration off his face and his neck, changes into informal Indian clothes, and makes his way to the dining room to eat lunch alone.

I have a banana in my bag if you are hungry, says Rahul.

I can wait, she says. They are only about a quarter of an hour away from Calcutta, but the trains have a nasty habit of halting tantalizingly close to their destination for indefinite periods, probably due to congestion at the terminus. Today they are lucky, and the train sails smoothly into the railway station, she notices that it is just past two by the station clock and realizes that her watch has stopped working.

Would you like to go and eat somewhere? he asks.

Don't you have to rush off to your chambers?

I am not usually back this early on Fridays, so I do have a bit of time.

Let us go to the College Street Coffee House, she suggests. There must have been a time when he was a regular there, as she had been when she was a student at Presidency College across the road.

It is strange that you should have picked this place, he says as they stroll in. I used to see you here sometimes, sitting in your circle of friends. I knew who you were but you did not know me.

Why did you not come and introduce yourself?

I was too shy, I suppose.

I find that hard to believe.

You are right, it was not that. You see, it was as if you belonged to an entirely different world. You lived in that grand house behind the mysterious gates, your mother was an actress, your uncle had been a genius who had drowned abroad – it was said for the love of a woman.

For the love of a woman?

Could it not be so?

It's funny that we should be discussing his motives for drowning when he did not actually drown at all.

We did not know that then, says Rahul. His death was a great mystery to us, and we could not see you except in the shadow of that mystery, you sat with your classmates, and unlike the others, you never once looked around to see who else was there, whether anybody was admiring you from afar, whether there was anybody you especially liked the look of, you never once looked over the shoulders of your companions, or turned to the sound of any other voice.

What will you have? she asks, picking up the menu.

A chicken omelette, I think. And you?

I cannot decide. You know, I have not been here in almost ten years, she tells him. For her existence in Calcutta in the last two years has had very little continuity with her first twenty-three years in the city. She has phoned only the closest of her friends, visited them briefly at their homes, taken gifts for their children. But they have their own busy lives now, and the few who are not burdened with their commitments – like some of the men who have not married yet and live with their parents – seem not to have made much spiritual progress since their days together as undergraduates, she has not been eager to join them for nights of idiotic drunken revelry. She had thirsted so often while she was abroad for the good times they had shared, the afternoons that they had whiled away in this coffee house, and she had hoped, when she returned to Calcutta, that part of that routine would be re-established, to give her some ease within the stern course she had chosen. But this has not happened, and here she is now, for the first time since she returned, in the College Street Coffee House, so redolent of a phase of her life when she had been confident that she knew all that there was to know about the human condition. How snugly she had settled into the belief that the rest would simply be an elaboration upon the framework that she had already established, how happily unaware she was that it would all be blown to bits by one look from a man called Daniel Faraday, whom they had thought then to be the last person to see her uncle alive.

Debendranath Roy dreams that he has strewn rice upon the seashore for it to cook, but that the warm waves have turned it instead into sand. He wakes with a dull ache in his head, and sees from his wristwatch that it is almost five o'clock, he has slept for several hours and it has not refreshed him. Where is Niharika? he wonders, as the gatekeeper's wife sets down a tray of tea and biscuits on his bedside table and tells him that she has not yet returned. He remembers how, when she was a child, she would often march into his room to wake him up if she thought he was sleeping too late. She would bring him tea and other refreshments which she would mainly consume herself, perched at the foot of his bed, while he tried to shake himself free of his dreams. For the skinny little thing that she was she had an enormous apetite. She would plunge immediately into the details of the events of the morning as they had unfolded to her, a heady pot pourri of the trivial and the significant, of fact and fantasy, that he would inhale with delight, as he slowly reconstituted himself between sips of strong sugary tea.

One of her obsessions at the time, which she shared with her brothers, was the story of the discovery of the source of the Nile, and she would often ask him if he had seen the river. He and Jennifer had stopped briefly in Cairo on their way back to Calcutta, but had had only enough time to dash to the pyramids before it got dark, so had not seen the Nile, he would tell her, and she would suck in her lower lip vexedly – not even a glimpse? she would ask.

He knew that her brothers did not always let her join them

in their game of enacting the drama of the discovery of the source of the Nile, even though she was content to take the humbler roles, and so she would have to do it all on her own, taking on the whole cast turn by turn. Debendranath Roy had watched her once as she valiantly trooped up and down the stairs, in and out of the various rooms, switching between Richard Burton and John Hanning Speke, and then she disappeared into the old storeroom where she liked to play, and did not come out for a while. He had been sorting through a crate of old papers at one end of the corridor, his presence had not interfered with her make-believe, and he had found himself pleasantly diverted at intervals from his task by her movements. After she had failed to emerge from the storeroom for a good half hour, he felt the need to follow her, and tiptoeing in through the maze of old furniture, he found her, in the solar topee and khaki trousers she had borrowed with permission from her brothers, crying quietly as she bandaged up the arms and legs of her dolls. She turned around at the sound of his feet, and quickly wiped away her tears. He knelt down and held out his right hand.

Dr Livingstone, I presume, he said.

I am afraid I should get back, says Rahul. My patients will be waiting.

The afternoon has glided by. They have sat in the Coffee House and talked for hours, and afterwards poked about in the roadside bookstalls, and then just walked through the rotting tapestry of alleys that they had roamed as students, but never with each other. Would her life have been different if she had met him then, she wonders, or would she have dismissed him as just another medical student with artistic inclinations. Who knows?

What is more important is that her life may change now quite irrevocably because of him, it is too soon to think so, but how can she help it, as she drinks in his words and gestures, pieces him together from the stories that he tells. The earnestness of their exchange is tinged with the candour of lovemaking, the desperate need to lay bare the soul before divesting the body of its wrappings, the need to delight in common goals and to rake out differences of opinion before entering into a concourse where nothing of that sort is likely to matter, the need to establish faith and hope before progressing to love.

And now they are sitting in the ice cream parlour close to their homes where they have decided to refresh themselves after their long walk, I have just enough time for a quick ice cream, he had said as they approached the shop. It is an ugly little place, he had said, but the ice cream is quite delicious. And ugly it was indeed, inexpertly modelled to suit a generation of youngsters who saw life in smalltown United States as the apotheosis of being, but the ice cream, as Rahul had promised, was good and came with such bald labels of the culture they were attempting to emulate that it made them cry with laughter. They have sat with their empty ice cream glasses for over an hour, and as the lights are switched on in the shop, Rahul fearfully consults his watch, and then tells her that he can dally no longer in her company, duty calls, duty lovingly calls, but he will see her again he hopes, before she leaves.

He walks her to the gates of her house. Are you doing anything tomorrow evening? he asks. If not, perhaps you would like to come to my rehearsal with me?

I would be delighted, she says.

I will call for you around six o'clock then, he says.

He waits for the gatekeepr to shut the gates behind her and then waves goodbye, she smiles in return and watches him disappear into the young evening, then she turns and walks towards the house. She finds her uncle in the drawing room, listening to a scratchy 78 rpm record of Tagore songs, *rid me of this mantle of obsession*, pleads the singer, and Debendra-nath Roy, unaware that she is standing at the door, whispers to the darkness, how could I have forgotten you? how could I have forgotten you? He buries his face in his hands, and she waits until the tender moment passes to announce her presence with a jingle of her bracelets, *let me drink my fill of your beauty, rid me of this mantle of obsession,* he turns around to see her darkly outlined in the doorway, and it is as if he sees not her but the silhouette of his lost beloved, but the illusion is brief, and he does not ask as she fears, is it you, can it be you? Instead he says, you must be very tired, how was the trip?

May I turn on the light? she asks.

Of course, he says. I should not be sitting in the dark anyway. God knows I will have enough of it in the days to come. I should enjoy my sight while I can.

In his hands is a book on Bohemian glass. I was reading, he tells her, and then I was rather overcome by these songs, I have hardly noticed that night has fallen for I have been listening with my eyes closed, one pleasure that my blindness will not deny me.

They hear a low cough, it is the gatekeeper, he looks tired, as if the sequence of events has worn him out, he approaches Debendranath Roy. Your wife is here, he says.

They hear the rusty gates being dragged open again by one of the servants, and the crunch of gravel as the taxi drives into the portico.

So she has come, says Debendranath Roy.

Niharika walks out onto the verandah to greet Jennifer. She is standing with her suitcase upon the stairs. Do you have any money, she asks her, the taxi driver does not want to accept pound coins.

She instructs the gatekeeper, who has followed her out, to pay the taxi driver, and leads the dazed Jennifer up the stairs. He is here, isn't he? she asks. He hasn't disappeared again, has he?

He may not want to see you straight away, she warns.

But Debendranath Roy has not left his seat, the book on Bohemian glass is open upon his lap, he raises his eyes towards his wife, hello Jennifer, he says, it is good of you to have come right away.

Jennifer stands in the doorway, shaking with sobs. Niharika wishes to leave, to let the two of them sort out their peculiar domestic drama, she wants to leave them here and sit alone in her room and ruminate upon the day's events, but she fears that Jennifer may collapse if she lets go of her. As if he senses her desire to leave, Debendranath Roy rises from his chair, walks over to where they stand and relieves her of her burden, he takes Jennifer by the hand and leads her to the sofa, sit down, he says, would you like a glass of water, or some tea?

I think she needs a drink, says Niharika.

Is there any alcohol in this house? asks her uncle.

I have been drinking rum, she says. But I know there is some brandy somewhere, the gatekeeper will know.

And so he is summoned again, and told to locate the old bottle of brandy while Niharika gets a maid to heat some milk. The mixture, she feels, might revive Jennifer. It was what she drank in the evenings she was not with Morgan, that winter in Princeton, after Daniel Faraday had left her with the promise that he would not interfere with her life easily again.

The gatekeeper finds the brandy in the old medicine chest still stuffed with the ayurvedic potions that Indranath Roy had consumed in the fierce hope that it might rid him of the cancer that had started to grow in his body soon after his younger son had quarrelled with him and left. Often, he had thought of writing to him to let him know that he might be dying, although he did not believe it himself, and the doctors were certain that it was in remission. Still, Indranath Roy had thought perhaps that the revelation that he had cancer might bring him back, but he was afraid that to use it as a fulcrum of their reconciliation might be to tempt fate, to tease it into taking over his body, as indeed it would within six months of the news that Debendranath Roy had drowned. They said that it was his broken heart that had aggravated the metastasis, but the gatekeeper knew that this was not true, the gatekeeper who had attended him in the hour of his death and in the many hours of his suffering that preceded it, knew that his will to live had not been dulled in the least by the news of his younger son's death.

I owe you an explanation, says Debendranath Roy to his wife, after she has taken a few sips of the warm milk and brandy, and composed herself somewhat.

I would rather not hear it, she says.

You are right, he says, you should rest now. We can talk later. Now is not the right time to explain my actions.

Not now, nor ever, she says with a determination that he had not imagined she might ever possess, twenty years ago, when he had sheltered her under his broken wing.

Do you mean that you never want to know?

I have learnt that some things are best left unexplored, she says, with a flicker of pride in her voice at this achievement.

Very well, then, we shall never speak of it again.

I just want you to come back with me, she says. I just want you to let me take care of you.

I may very well do that, says Debendranath Roy.

CRIMSON

It has been beastly hot, he writes, and we are all relieved that the monsoon has arrived, but it has brought in its wake the usual kaleidoscope of disease, and I can hardly ever get away from the village clinic until it is almost dark, then I am usually so late for rehearsals that they have dropped me from the main role and assigned to me a much smaller part – for which I am actually grateful, for quite honestly I do not have the energy to play Creon.

He has written to her almost every week since she left Calcutta, found time in his busy day to sit down at his desk and compose a letter in his transculent Tagorean prose, and with each letter she has found herself more and more entranced by his lack of artifice, the clear lattice of his thoughts. It is not as if Rahul Mitra does not have his own mystery, but the solid simplicity with which he speaks of his slightly surreal existence fills her with a marvellous ease, with every letter it has become clearer to her that she would willingly return to take her place by his side, if that is where he wants her. Together they could revive Mandalay, perhaps turn one of its wings into a clinic for the poor. She has even thought of having a few beds in it, but she knows she would never want to live among the sick and the dying, and neither, she feels, would he.

It has been almost a year since she left Calcutta, and soon she will have to decide whether she stays in Oxford on a three-year fellowship she has been offered at her old college, or whether she goes back. She looks in Rahul's letters for some indication that he is waiting for her, and although it boldly declares how deeply he values her, how grateful he is to have embarked upon this tender and honest epistolary relationship, it is not within the radius of his prose to disclose his passionate desire to be with her. She has offered him a cue in her last letter by laying out her dilemma in some depth, the temptation of being cossetted within a college environment and left to conduct her life without the need to cook and clean for herself, and the same advantages in Calcutta, but without the stimulation of an academic environment. Not a contradiction in terms anymore to her, she had hastened to explain, for she had left him last with the impression that she found academia quite stultifying. In this last year, from her new, slightly detached position as a writer in residence, she had come to appreciate the company of individuals so deeply immersed in their particular subject of study. It was a way to live and it worked, she had reasoned, it was not unpleasant to be surrounded by those who had chosen it as their path to the grave. She has written to him covertly begging for some sign of the depth of his affection, and now his reply has arrived, and the first few pages are of the news that the rains have come, a little early, but hardly too soon. She reads rapidly through them, and then scans his observations on the current state of political affairs, and finally finds, in his last paragraph, what she has been hoping for, I hope you will decide to return, he has written, for I have been waiting breathlessly for the day, and it will be a great blow to me if it is delayed for another three years. I will carry on of course as I always do, and three years will no doubt pass quite rapidly, and the stream of letters back and forth I hope will not wither, but it will be hard to imagine, after a while, that you will come back at all.

In the year that she has been in Oxford, little else has happened in her life besides the sweet stream of the letters from Rahul. Debendranath Roy has been reinstalled in the house by the railway station, where he keeps in Braille the accounts of the Bed & Breakfast that his wife still runs. He has lived for almost six months now under the same roof that sheltered him when he first came to Oxford, thirty years ago. His sight has left him more rapidly than they had expected, sometimes she suspects that it is because he would rather not see how it has all ended, in case the full circle becomes a noose, if it already is not. She has seen a lot of him and Jennifer since they returned from Calcutta, where they had been forced to stay much longer than she had planned on account of the formalities of reviving his civic status, re-establishing his right to return to Britain and reside there indefinitely as her husband. Jennifer had not dared to return without him, in case he disappeared again, indeed every morning she would breathe a sigh of relief to find him at the breakfast table, for they did not share a room in Mandalay, nor indeed do they now.

Rahul Mitra had inquired after him regularly during the time Debendranath Roy spent in Calcutta. They would play chess together on the evenings when he was not rehearsing, or still sitting on a delayed passenger train on his way back from the village clinic. He did not seem to find it peculiar that he had returned from his twenty-year exile on account of his impending blindness, it was no more ruthless than the decisions he took every day about people's lives, weighing their sufferings against the needs of others, and the resources that were collectively available to them, coldly evaluating their options and trying to steer them towards what he saw as the right course of action.

He had reported to her about her uncle's condition. In simple clinical detail, he had informed her of the state of his eyes, which were quite stable at the time, and of whether he still seemed comfortable about returning to England. But in this Rahul's opinion was coloured by his own viewpoint which was that he should remain in Calcutta in the house that he knew and loved, where he would be taken care of by faithful servants and the vast network of relatives. Besides, he could revive his old connections, his friends from college, the members of the film society to which he had belonged in his youth, Rahul even suggested that he join their theatre group, there was a whole array of possibilities for the roles that he could play, other than the obvious ones like Tiresias and

Tagore's King of the Hidden Chamber. Drama is the best therapy, he had assured Niharika.

I am not sure it had quite that effect on my mother, she had said with some bitterness.

Your mother had too much of an effect on everything else for anything to have an effect upon her. That was her tragedy, he had said.

And Niharika had remembered then how she had come upon her a few years ago, during her parents' visit to Oxford, sitting upon the patch of green beside Hythe Bridge with her granddaughter, when she had felt that she was spying upon a queen reflecting upon her sorrows in a private corner of her vast gardens, the little area had been transformed by her presence, the willow across the river seemed to be weeping at her feet. And now she realized that because everything had converged upon her, her mother had learnt nothing from sitting by the narrow canal, because she had illuminated everything, nothing ever shone its truth upon her.

It was difficult being her daughter, she had told Rahul.

But deeply rewarding, no doubt.

More so now, she had replied. In the two years that she had lived in Calcutta, her mother had never visited her, but she had arranged for them to meet, a couple of times, for a few days at a hotel in the hills or by the sea. It was as if she too was avoiding the great house where she had once been mistress, now an ocean of decay. But she had never questioned like the others why Niharika might want to live there, indeed a different kind of understanding had grown between them, and the short holidays that they had taken together had been pleasant if always rather serious, she had never learnt to laugh with her mother, it was not a hurdle they were ever likely to cross.

In this final season of her ripeness, she was more beautiful than ever, the rich grey of her hair framing her fine features, her gaze streaked with hard gold, and her bearing never more regal. A formidable hush seemed to descend upon the forests of pine and cedar as she walked in stately silence through them with her daughter, and when upon the seashore she burst into song, the waves would foam in awe at her feet. She was still as aloof to strangers, but now she seemed more distracted than dismissive, not that it would have mattered anymore to Niharika, who had once so resented Reba's indifference to her schoolfriends. Their mothers were always so chatty and informal, whereas her mother treated her friends with a reserve that was close to scorn. It was a relief that she was almost never there when she invited them home after school.

She had often wondered what it would be like to have a mother who was a friend to her, to whom she could repeat bits of school gossip, confess obliquely her crushes on young men, a mother who would consult her about the saris and shawls she purchased, advise her about her own choice of clothes. On a few occasions Reba had tried to teach her how to prepare an unusual dish in her private kitchen, but even in this her manner had been no less grave than while giving her a music lesson. It would have hurt her less if she had felt that her mother was incapable of frivolity, but she had seen her laugh and make merry in the company of others, especially in her grandfather's flat, surrounded by his friends and minions who all knew her to possess a superb sense of humour. She seemed to be perfectly capable of teasing her sons at times, especially about their devotion to their hobbies and schoolfriends, it was only with her daughter that Reba did not know how to joke. It was as if they were frozen in the solemnity that an adult affects with a very young child, careful not to make light of their desperate attempts to understand and classify the world around them. That was, after all, the only period in her life when her mother had been occupied with her, before she turned three and started to go to nursery school and Reba was gradually consumed by her involvements in music and the theatre. By the time her uncle returned with his new English wife, she hardly saw her mother during the day at all. She found a new companion in Jennifer, and for a while the journey home from school had been filled with the marvellous anticipation of seeing her and wondering what new activities she may have devised for them that day. The gatekeeper would grumble that he could not keep up with her as she skipped back across the broken pavements, and he laboured behind with her schoolbag and waterbottle. Jennifer had brought her a small jointed teddy bear from England. It was the first stuffed animal that anyone had given her, even though her toy cupboard was crowded with dolls of all shapes and sizes. She would insist that the gatekeeper brought the bear with him when he met her at the schoolgates, so that she could walk back home with him in her arms. One rainy day, she had dropped him in a puddle and cried all the way home, Jennifer had helped her bathe him carefully in soap and hot water, but he had taken ages to dry and smelt a little mildewed for a long time afterwards. She had brought the teddy bear with her to Oxford, and Jennifer had been so moved to see it perched upon the windowsill in her bedroom that tears had come to her eyes.

After we came back to England, she said to Niharika, whenever I saw something you would have liked I was seized by a desperate urge to buy it for you and send it to you. Sometimes I thought of sending it without telling your uncle, but I was afraid your mother would return it with a curt note. He would never have forgiven me then. Now I think that perhaps he would not have minded so much if I had sent something to you, but of course I never had the courage to ask.

She remembered that when the grown-ups had gone to parties, it was always Jennifer who had smuggled back pastries and cakes for them. Her mother clearly disapproved of this. It's not as if they don't get such things at home, she would tell Jennifer. But it seemed to Niharika that what mattered more to her mother was the indignity of the act. She did not want her children to enjoy food that had been concealed in a handbag.

It is hard to eat knowing that they might be hungry, Jennifer had once said in her defence, when Niharika and her twin brothers had been waiting in a car outside. There had been some misunderstanding, and the children had found that they were not invited, Reba had told them to wait while she and Jennifer made a token appearance, but within the half hour that they spent there, Jennifer had excused herself and dashed out to the car with a pile of sandwiches sloppily hidden under her shawl. How could I eat knowing that they were sitting starving in the car, she had protested later.

They are never so hungry that they cannot wait for half an hour, Reba had replied.

If life had been harder for them, would her mother have been more tender, Niharika sometimes wonders, would her mother have respected her more if she had not been born into such privilege, if she had been forced like her to use public transport to travel to college, or like her trembled with fear when a storm laid her *esraj* flat upon the ground, knowing that if it was cracked they could not afford to mend it until her father received his next months' salary. She wonders now, sometimes, if her marriage into their family had not been to her mother a deal with the devil, a means of deliverance from the tedium of living within their means. Not that her grandfather did not earn enough to feed and clothe his family reasonably well, pay his wife's medical bills and still keep one or two servants, buy books and records, provide his daughter with the best music tuition. It was not as if she was denied anything she really needed, but the notion of being able to pursue her interests, indulge in her refinements without the constraint of money must have appealed to her. Why else would she have submitted to an arranged marriage with the eldest son of a family of businessmen who had recently made a fortune in Burma teak?

It had struck her at a very young age that there was something very different from Mandalay about the atmosphere of her grandfather's flat. There the books that crowded and spilled from the many open shelves seemed to breathe their own life. Each book had its place but it was like an old address upon a street, whereas in her home the books marched in alphabetical order behind polished glass, even in her mother's room. They seemed hardly more important than the marquetry upon the bookcases. It was in her grandfather's flat that she came to love books, simply for the smell of them if nothing else appealled to her among the pages, but more often it was not just the smell, for there was an entire unruly ocean to drink of between the covers, just the act of thumbing the pages had for her an intensely sensual thrill, it was only in writing a book of her own that she had ceased to love them as much.

Even now, when occasionally she is overcome by nostalgia, it is the fragrance of her grandfather's flat that she inhales most strongly, it is the only truly holy space that she has known, save perhaps Morgan's flat in New York, where nothing was for decoration, and yet everything radiated grace. She remembers how she would rest against his leather armchair while he played Schubert on his baby grand piano, death and the maiden crashing over the keys. It was the closest she had ever come to receiving absolution. But then he would stop suddenly, and his face would contort in agony – the fucking bass, he would shriek, it always sounds like it's coming out of an elephant's arsehole – and then he would spend hours fussing around inside it with a feathered stick as if the tone could be altered for him by the weight of dust upon the strings, where was he now, Morgan, would she ever see him again?

And Daniel Faraday? To him she is simply grateful for releasing her from the silent vow that they would belong to each other forever. Nothing else had seemed possible at the time, and to think that it is no longer the same fills her with as much sorrow as relief. Has she really lost him forever, or simply discovered a way to accommodate him without disturbing the balance of her life. For in vain had she been beset by the terrible fear that she would be overwhelmed by memories of their passion as soon as she set foot in Oxford. In vain had she agonized how they might scorch the green shoots of her tenderness towards Rahul Mitra. It had not happened, but in not happening much of the landscape that she loved had been robbed of meaning, the cobbled streets no longer throbbed with the anguish of their love, the river flowed treacherously happy, and the curve of the hills no longer invited her to lay upon them her aching head, the trees grew fingers that pointed to other diffuse heavens, had she really lost him then, lost him forever?

Perhaps that was her true reason for wishing to go. When a place loses its colour – what earthly reason can there be to stay? And today, knowing this, she hopes that at least once before she bids farewell, she may be drenched by the memory of his kisses, yearn just once for his embrace, or simply to be seated across from him at a table, drinking in his presence, hearing his laughter, feeling his eyes upon her, noticing how he twists the plain wedding band upon his finger, the veins upon his hands as he taps the base of his wineglass, the flash of his shoe under the tablecloth as it edges dangerously close to her and then, sensing her sublime distress, slowly withdraws.

She buys flowers from a vendor outside the Westgate Arcade to take to Jennifer. She has eaten many of her meals there since they returned from Calcutta. It is exactly as Jennifer had wistfully imagined it could have been if her husband had been alive, just after Niharika had first arrived in Oxford and had plunged with great gusto into the business of being an international student here, giving Jennifer the impression that she did not have that much time for her faded forty year old aunt. She had felt, at the time, that things would have been vastly different if Debendranath Roy had still been alive, that they would have much to talk about, and it would be a relief to Niharika anyway to be able to speak in Bengali, and she would quietly remove herself, as she does now, to give them this freedom. There is nothing so sweet to her now as the sound of them talking to each other in their own language, as she cooks dinner or hauls the laundry down into the cellar. It is a dream come true and for this she never ceases to give thanks. She has always been religious, but going to mass every Sunday morning had only become a firm habit since she moved to Oxford and took over the boarding house. Every Sunday morning, after she had served breakfast to the B&B guests, she would walk to the Oratory on Woodstock Road to attend the eleven o'clock mass, and then afterwards she would buy the Sunday paper to take home, or if it was a warm summer day, to the University Parks, where she would sit and read it and then feed the ducks before coming back home for lunch.

It was a worry to her that Debendranath Roy might disapprove of her going to church when they returned to Oxford six months ago, for he had been extremely censorious about it as a young man. But she had no reason to be anxious. Not only did he not disapprove, but lately had begun to accompany her to mass, where he would sit relishing the incense and the music, and the loftiness of the vaulted ceiling which was no longer within the compass of his sight. It made her uneasy that his reasons were not the same as hers for being there, and she wished at times that he would not come, but it was nice to walk back with him leaning upon her arm, to stop at the French bakery for almond croissants and other extravagances that she would never have felt before that she could afford. But now her whole life seemed to lift in the praise of the moment, her good fortune seemed to justify all imprudence. She has plans to spend some of her savings redecorating their living area, put in another door to seal it off more completely, give it the feel of a self-contained flat.

I am getting the gas fire replaced, she tells Niharika as they drink a glass of wine in the living room before lunch. I am getting them to put in the sort of fire that looks like a real fire but runs off gas, she announces. I know how much you have always hated it, she says to her husband.

My dear, it will hardly make a difference to me, says Debendranath Roy.

Oh it will, she says, it's nice to feel the heat from a real flame.

I am sure you will feel the difference, says Niharika in support of her aunt.

Well, if it is as they say that my powers of discrimination will grow in proportion to my blindness, I may soon be able to tell between the warmth of a gas fire and that which burns real coal or wood, says Debendranath Roy.

Besides, I still have my eyes, submits Jennifer.

Indeed you do. What would I do without them? he says, patting her affectionately on her elbow, as she brings a dish of olives into the penumbra of his failing vision, the grey circle that tightens a little every day.

He is more at ease with his blindness than Niharika ever expected he would be, the blindness that brought him out of his hiding and rotated him ironically into the same position he had unilaterally renounced so many years ago. There are many advantages to being in this country, he says, they know how to cater to the blind. Soon he will have a dog to guide him around town. He has mastered Braille with the same greed that he showed for foreign languages when he was young. A university student comes to read to him in the afternoon, and sometimes in the evening Niharika has been reading to him from her book, it is written from the perspective of a daughter he might have had, a child that he might have left behind, who would have been taken to live in Calcutta with his family after his death. She had been reluctant to read to him of himself as she had seen him before he became real to her, but he had told her that he would not be able to bear it being read to him by anyone else, and since he could not see enough to read it on his own anymore, she would be depriving him of it altogether if she refused him his request. It nestles now against the catalogue of fireplaces upon the glass-topped coffee table where Jennifer often leaves it to show proudly to visitors. She has not read it yet herself, perhaps afraid of how it might affect her. Niharika can hardly blame her, it is not easy to read from it to her uncle.

These olives are particularly moreish, are they not? says Debendranath Roy.

They are quite delicious, she agrees.

Jennifer gets them from the covered market, he tells her. Can you give me an ashtray or something for the pips?

She fetches him a malachite ashtray that Jennifer must have acquired on one of the trips she had started to take to rather exotic places with her group of women friends, most of them divorced or single, a few with husbands almost totally indifferent to their existence, and her the only widow. Since Debendranath's return, they have prudently left her alone. She has enough on her hands, they tell her, with a blind husband to look after. Occasionally, she goes out for a drink with them, after extracting from him the promise that he will not do anything rash, but she always itches to return, even though she knows he is happy, perhaps happier, on his own.

A journalist from a woman's magazine telephoned today, he tells Niharika. They want to interview me, as the character in your new book, who came back from the dead and turned it all into a lie.

Did you agree to the interview? she asks.

Giving interviews is one of the few things I can do now, he tells her.

So you will do it?

Do you object?

Of course not, she says. I am just interested in the idea that you challenged the truth of my work of fiction by appearing in the flesh.

Are you writing anything else? he asks.

I have nothing to write, she says. I am not sure I ever will have anything more to write, which is partly why I feel I should not accept the fellowship I have just been offered.

You are going away then, he says with a sad smile.

I think so, she says.

It is that young doctor, is it not? He is drawing you back into the shadows where you never thought you would belong, not since you looked out of your bedroom window as a child and saw the streets crowded, not with people, but their rustling husks.

I have not quite made up my mind, she tells him.

Then let me make it up for you, says Debendranath Roy. Let me be the one to urge you to return to that rotting paradise, let me be the one to remind you of the smell of new rain upon baked earth, the brutally honest call of the carrion crow, the glory of the red evening as it sinks into its muddy reflection in the communal pond, the march of a mother with her child to his school through the midmorning fury of the sun, his khaki satchel stretched across his thin shoulders and his water bottle bobbing up and down in his hands, let me be the one to bring back to you the scent of the michelia flower, its maddeningly subtle yellow, that I am grateful to be able to recapture in my blindness, for I will never see it again but in my mind's eye. You will never find it anywhere except there, in the land where you were born.

These are as good reasons as any, but they are not enough to make me return.

No, he says, of course not. You will return because of the young doctor, because there are few men that you have met with his strength of purpose, unburdened as it is by the noise of conscience. There is no one that you have met with his diversity of talent, or at least no one who puts them to such good use without agonizing over how to mete himself out into his many roles, in this respect he appears to be quite remarkable, and even if he does not prove to be, you will be united, as men and women are in the shadow of war and natural calamity, by struggling to cope with the pain around you.

You speak with the the tongue of angels, she says.

But I have no gift of prophecy, he says. If I had I would not have pretended to drown in the Cherwell twenty-one years ago, says Debendranath Roy.

After lunch, she tells her aunt, while they are doing the dishes, that she has decided to return to Calcutta.

I hope it is for a very good reason, says Jennifer.

I met a man just before I left last year, we have been writing to each other since then.

That is just what I was hoping you would say.

You may know him, she tells her. I believe he used to come and play chess with my uncle in Calcutta in the months that you were stranded there.

Yes, I remember him, says Jennifer. He seemed a very nice young man although I never really got to know him. Your uncle was always impatient to start the game, and I would usually creep away rather than sit there in silence and watch.

I wonder who usually won, she says smiling.

Your uncle will miss you, says Jennifer.

I will miss him.

Perhaps you can both come and live in Oxford, her aunt says hopefully.

That is not likely to happen, she replies.

Has he a very good job there?

It is more that he is devoted to his work there – which is among the poor. He is a doctor you see.

Speaking of him and his work fills her with a comforting warmth, like settling into a nest of blankets with a good book and a glass of wine, but it is not devoid of a sense of excitement, there is so much that they might do together, she is certain that he is full of wonderful ideas, about how to dispense cheap medical care, about writing a play together, about where they might travel and what they might eat and drink. She feels impatient to discuss them with him. She will write him a long letter as soon as she returns to her rooms in college, to end the suspense for him and for herself about whether she will return at the end of the summer.

Are you in a hurry, asks her uncle, when she emerges from the kitchen, are you in a rush or do you have time to read a little of your book before you leave?

I should love to read some of it to you now, she says, for although she itches to return to her rooms and compose the letter to Rahul, she also knows that she will never forgive herself if she does not finish the book before she leaves.

He hands her the book, which he has been holding in his hands, running his hands over its strange cover with a photograph of a figure disappearing into the mist. Niharika begins to read: *A week after my father disappeared into the Cherwell, my grandfather came to fetch us, at the same boarding house where my parents had met, where we were sheltered now by my mother's aunt, a wretched widow and her child. You could finish your librarianship course, my mother's aunt suggested to her, you could stay here and help around the place meanwhile, you and the girl. You'd have to earn your keep, she said to me, waggling a finger, as if half in jest, you're a big girl now, you can make yourself of some use. Which is perhaps how I came to be vacuuming the hallway when, a few hours later, she opened the door to my grandfather. His first glimpse of me was a small red face struggling to push a decrepit Hoover across a mothcoloured rug, I am your grandfather, he told me immediately, I have come to take you home. My mother, wearing her new bereavement like a piece of shapeless sacking, greeted him with confusion, there is no body, she told him, once he had been allowed to wash his hands and been given a cup of tea. Of course there is no body, my grandfather replied. I haven't come for the body, I have come for my son's child, and his widow, you must come back with me to Calcutta. This is like Charles Dickens, I thought, behind my jam doughnut. My father's death had not caught up with me yet, my mother's grief was too thin and frantic, like grey candyfloss. I had brushed it aside, scraped away the sticky tufts that clung nonetheless to my small fingers. After all, I had been told that he had simply gone away for a while, that someday he would return, someday he would find the key of his flying casket, and fly straight back to us, meanwhile he was forced to languish in some strange kingdom faraway, so I told* my cousin, on my first night in Calcutta, as we lay together in the dark, but she only rolled away to the other end of the vast bed, muttering – I don't believe you, I don't believe you at all, said my cousin.

My father is a wizard, I insisted to her, he has gone away to a different galaxy, on a very special adventure, he will tell us all about it when he comes back. I don't believe you, she said, rolling away into the treacly dark, I don't believe you at all. We woke with the sun beating upon our faces, and then washed and brushed, but still in our nightdresses we came down to her mother's apartments, where she was waiting, freshly bathed and smelling of sandalwood, with a special breakfast of puffed bread and potato curry, laid out in neat stainless steel dishes, between tall tumblers of warm milk for us to drink with our meal. She had her own tiny kitchen. Although the main meals were all prepared by the cook in his vast dungeon, she liked to experiment with recipes, bake exotic cakes. For my ninth birthday she made a pair in the shape of two eyes, but my schoolfriends were more awed than amused, it's a shame to eat something so beautiful, they all said. Your friends have no sense of humour, my cousin told me later, they are no fun at all. We were at the same school, which was just down the road from where we lived, but she was four years older, and had exercise books for strange subjects like Algebra, and friends with whom she could stalk the musty school corridors in search of the source of the White Nile, if she so wished. Sometimes I was allowed to join them, on Tuesdays, when we both did afternoon French classes. Afterwards I might be recruited in the role of some factotum, shapeless identities that I would quietly endure, secure in the knowledge that when we replayed the adventure later in the veinous hallways of our home, just the two of us, I too would have the privilege of bursting upon her amid a crowd of old furniture and greet her with the cry: Dr Livingstone, I presume? Attached to the bedroom that we shared was a vast bathroom, no longer in use, teeming with discarded furniture, this was *where we would spend our afternoons, feeding upon each other's fantasies, threading them together into macabre romances, each of which we would enact for an audience of spiders and the ghosts of the family of Mr Atherton, from whom my grandfather had purchased the house. James Atherton's ghost, my cousin told me, visited regularly, although he had been buried on some wild English moor, what was a wild English moor, I wondered, my meagre acquaintance with the British wilderness came from long walks we took on Hampstead Heath, long sad walks, my mother tightly clutching my hand, desperately trying to surface from within her own miseries, even then we had nothing to say to each other, and already felt ashamed of this whiteribbed space between us. You are incapable of amusing the child, my father would accuse her, you have no imagination, you have no refinement of spirit, you may as well not exist, he had told her, he who himself the following summer would succumb to the temptation to cease to be, once and for all to chalk himself off the mortal register, he would take me often to the cemetery in Highgate, never be afraid of death, he told me, there is enormous dignity in death, he would say, this cemetery is one of the most beautiful places in London, my father would say, certainly one of the least morbid. I have seen James Atherton's grave in Highgate Cemetery, I lied to my cousin. He lies there under cracked stone with his wife and three sons, I told her. But his heart, she insisted, is buried in the dark soil of the Yorkshire moors, so that his spirit may wander unchecked among the hills and the vales with his lover, for that is where she is buried, his ravishing mistress, she was the wife of an army officer here, together they murdered his wife, here in this very room, she had said, drowned her in this bath, she had said, walking slowly towards the cracked clawed tub in the half trance that seemed to grip her often in the frenzy of fabrication, she had lowered herself into its pitted interior, spread her luxurious hair over the piled carcasses of moths, and pretended to drown, like the poor Mrs Atherton, to whom she had assigned this violent fate. I watched her as she lay freed from the heat of her imagination, perfectly still, in the old bathtub, her face like cooling porcelain in the slatted sunlight, death had never seemed so close to me ever as this, I ran to the window and flung open the shutters in the hope that the rage of the tropical afternoon would break her poise, that she would be returned to me from the realm of her dreams.*

Niharika looks up and sees that Debendranath Roy has fallen asleep, she gently puts the book down on the table beside him, and tiptoes out of the room. Jennifer is still tidying up in the kitchen, she tells her that he has dozed off, kisses her goodbye, and promises to drop by in the evening to read some more.

She starts to walk back towards the centre of town, it is a soft summer afternoon, and the world seems to buzz like a low pitched chorus of happy insects somewhere far away, she feels happy walking in the streets, halts before one of the antique shops that dot her way home, and enters it simply to wander among the pieces of old furniture, the alluring bric-a-brac. She purchases a painted egg which reminds her somehow of the enamelled box where her mother kept her sewing needles, she decides that she will send it to her in Delhi.

She cuts through the parking lot and makes her way past the bus station and the rash of faceless restaurants and stops to eat an ice cream for she feels that this is one of the things she will miss – coffee ice cream, sprinkled with chopped walnuts – perhaps she will learn to make her own, the possibilities for the rest of her life seem endless at this moment, and she stands in the crowd of Saturday shoppers, eating her tub of ice cream, and feels happy to be able to concentrate on its coldness upon her tongue without any other hugely significant thought competing with this sensation. Then she throws the empty tub away and crosses the street, lets herself into her college through a side door, and stops for a while to take in the gracious vista of the courtyard, she will miss this, she is tempted to walk for a while in the garden, but then she remembers that she wants to write to Rahul, and decides instead to go straight to her rooms.

She climbs up the narrow stairs to her rooms, someone is whistling the theme of 'The Threepenny Opera', it echoes down the curved stairwell and gladdens her for it seems to reaffirm her destiny, that her place in this world is with Rahul, that her fate had been sealed in that moment he appeared on stage in his silk gloves as Mack the Knife, for she had known then that his devotion to his trade and his art was deep enough to sustain him, and anyone he cared to drag along with him, for the rest of his life. She walks in a happy trance up the first flight of stairs, and then suddenly, as the whistling becomes more precise, she realizes that it is a familiar breath that is fashioning these notes, she turns the corner with her heart beating fast and finds Daniel Faraday resting upon her doorstep, Morgan has killed himself, he says.

Is that what brings you here? As a bearer of bad news, she manages to say, fumbling in her purse for her keys. When she finds them, she presses them deeply into her palm, wishing that they might make her bleed, her humble keys, stigmatize this moment upon her with their perfect uneven teeth.

No, that is not why I am here, he says, that is not why I am here.

Yesterday morning, I woke up and felt that you no longer belonged to me, he says. I could not bear it, I came straight here.

From Sydney? she asks.

That is why I am wearing winter clothes, he says.

And Morgan, when did he kill himself? she asks, tears pouring down her cheeks as she turns the key vainly in the lock.

About a year ago, he replies.

She begins to weep, her head against the metal studded door. A year ago? she says, a year ago?

Beloved, he pleads, forget Morgan. I am here now, you have not seen me since the very first day of this decade.

He pushes away her hair and kisses the back of her neck, let us go in, he says.

My keys don't seem to work, she says, it is a dodgy lock.

Then let us not go in, he says, let us go punting, as I promised you so many years ago.

But it is almost dusk, she says.

The river will not be so crowded then, he replies.

Whatever it is you fill me with, he says to her burying his face in her hair, it drains away very slowly, but when it is gone, I am driven absolutely mad.

And now you are here to drink of me again, she says.

Beloved, he says, do not be bitter, the truth of you and me is here and now, and not in the long days that you have spent without me, the fantastic few months with Morgan chasing your pygmy whom I disparaged so much, the agonizingly fulfilling time of writing your novel about him, the heady days that followed of your newborn fame, like a cloud of cheap racehorses around you, not worthless but easy to dismiss, and then your brief seclusion amid the grand decay of your childhood home, writing a novel whose protagonist has appeared resurrected in its wake.

Will you go to see him?

I am afraid he might disappear again if I do.

You credit much to your intrusion into other people's lives.

I have never thought that I was the cause of your uncle's disappearance.

But perhaps that you triggered something in him that cascaded eventually in a desire not to return to his old life.

Perhaps that, he admits. But he is back now in his old life, after an interval of twenty years.

Yes, he is back now, but he no longer has much of his sight.

So my mother tells me. But he and my father can still discuss the geometry of the universe beside the fire, each with a warm tumbler of brandy in his hands, perhaps he even sees it better now, the intricate topology of the surface of a dying star, in his new blindness, your uncle.

He pushes her against the door of a broom closet on the same landing and kisses her upon her lips, he tries the handle and finds that it opens, I have not made love in a cupboard since I was a teenager, he says.

I do not want to make love, she says.

Because of Morgan? he asks. Have I plunged you into a state of mourning with the news of his death?

Indeed you have, she says. But that is not why I feel I must resist you. It is because if I do not, I will be betraying an honest man who loves me, whom I have given reason to believe I love him.

He continues to kiss her but his hand drops away from the handle of the closet door. You will come punting with me, though? he asks.

I cannot deny you the opportunity to fulfil such an old promise, she replies.

Tell me you want me to take you down the river, he pleads, just tell me that.

I do not need to tell you anything, she says, you know my heart.

And within the meshes of his waking darkness, Debendranath Roy dreams of Mandalay again, dreams that somewhere in that great house a spiderweb is gently falling, somewhere in that great house a spiderweb is falling under the fine weight of its own dust, somewhere among those unswept corridors the shed skins of their small histories are gathering for a great storm, and the old gatekeeper, grass sprouting green beneath his fingers, he is piling his broken pots within the gatehouse, before the skies break and his unglazed vessels melt into red mud.

Before he helps her into the boat, Daniel Faraday gives her a small parcel, wrapped in brown paper and clumsily embellished with a green ribbon.

What have you brought me this time? she asks.

Do you still have the boatshaped brooch?

You want me to tell you that I sleep with it under my pillow, don't you?

But you do not.

I have not looked at it in a long time, she confesses. Whenever I do, it disappoints me, because I expect to be transported into the ecstasy of that afternoon when you gave it to me, and that never happens, perhaps I am not the sort of person who can attach a memory more strongly to a precious object than to herself.

Perhaps this one will be more evocative.

She unwraps the brown paper as he pushes gently off the shore. It is an old scrapbook filled with cuttings related to the mysterious disappearance of an Indian schoolteacher, Debendranath Roy, whose body was never found in the Cherwell where he was presumed to have drowned. The tabloids had picked up the story and distorted in ways that she would never have been capable of while she was writing her book, she has to credit them with more imagination than herself, and he, Daniel Faraday, had cut out these titillating flights of fancy and pasted them alongside the more serious but rather bland reports of the incident.

You should have sent these to me before I wrote the book, she says.

Surely that would have been disastrous.

In any case, it is a present that you should have given him rather than me.

I thought about it, but then I decided it would be of more value to someone more intent on reinventing him than himself.

Debendranath Roy dreams that a storm is sweeping through the halls of Mandalay, ripping the curtains from their rusty rails, blowing the shutters off their toothless hinges, raising a tornado of old mothwings in the linen closets. Reba's musical instruments huddle together in their shapeless jackets as the wind knocks them dangerously together, photograph frames start to collapse face down upon the dressers, the pots and pans in her old kitchen tremble as the doors to her drawing room fly open. You are not dying are you? he asks her, in his dream, let me see you once more before you leave this earth, except I cannot see now, and will have to touch your face, to run my fingers over its lineaments, as I had once hardly dared to imagine, let me feel you near me just once before you go, if it is your death that this wind speaks of, this great wind that is ripping out my heart.

But then he knows it is not so, for she has passed outside the periphery of his premonition a long time ago. He has no sense of the texture of her life now, as the mother of a successful businessman in New Delhi, as the grandmother of three children who speak English to each other and communicate with her in broken Bengali, he has seen her on holiday with them, sedately occupying her position of honour, and from a distance he has felt that she was lavishing upon them an affection that she never gave her children. He had seen her in her life as it was now, but he could neither taste nor feel it, let alone be moved by the presentiment of her death, how could I have forgotten her? he asks himself. How could I have forgotten her?

I have something else for you, says Daniel Faraday, holding the boat still for a while, and reaching into his pocket for a box, which he tosses carefully in her direction.

She catches it in both hands and knows even before she opens it that it is the locket that Morgan so loved of the lyre made out of Keats' hair.

He left it to you, says Daniel, I have been meaning to send it to you for a long time.

You are lying, she says.

I am, he agrees.

He left it to you?

And everything else.

His entire fortune?

All of what he was worth. I have not done anything about it, no one knows, not even Alison.

So you could disappear with it if you liked and never be heard of again.

Oh, she would track me down, she is very efficient at that sort of thing, although it might be that she would not want to find me anymore, he says.

He takes the bend in the river that will take them further out along its course rather than turning to make the circle that would bring them back before dark to the point where they hired the boat.

Will it not be rather late before we return if we go this way? she asks.

We can always turn back, he replies.

But you would rather go on, she says, putting the locket back in its case.

She leans back upon her elbows and tilts her head up to look into his eyes.

I could go on like like this forever, he says.

It is getting a little chilly for me.

He throws her his overcoat which is lying at his feet. Wrap your lovely self in this, he says.

She feels a lump in one of the pockets, it is a miniature bottle of vodka from his aeroplane flight, I thought I might need it while I was waiting for you, he explains, I envisaged myself keeping vigil outside the library steps as I used to when I felt like surprising you, so many years ago.

I have not lost the habit of looking around for you, she says, whenever I emerge from the library, or indeed anywhere else. Perhaps that was why I was not as surprised as I should have been to see you upon my doorstep today.

But it was, of course, when you were least expecting me?

I do not know that. All I know is that I felt I was ready to try perhaps not to look for you in every crowd, not to wake up every morning and hope that you might be waiting outside.

And who would you look for instead? he asks.

No one. I thought I might exchange illusion for certainty.

In the shape of?

I met a man, about a year ago, he is a doctor, committed to his work among the rural poor, and in his spare time he is an actor.

Like your mother?

It is perhaps not quite such a passion for him. He is not desperately seeking, like her, to make sense of his life.

That's a relief, says Daniel Faraday.

You sound as if you are mocking me, she protests.

I suppose I am mocking you, he admits. What else can I do when you tell me you are about to replace me in your heart with someone else?

I did not say so, she tells him. That was not what I said at all. I simply felt, this afternoon, that I could perhaps rest the bulk of my life upon the bedrock of an honest pact between myself and him to love and trust each other, to entertain and look after one another, to allow the delightful urge to be in each other's company burgeon into a merry lust, which would drain away in due course, but not without leaving us the luxury of a robust pleasure in making love, I thought I might be able to treasure you within this somehow, as you had sheltered me in your life, with more care and less anguish, these were my thoughts as I came up the stairs and found you, whistling to yourself upon my doorstep.

Oh, the shark has pretty teeth dear, and he shows them a pearly white, just a jack-knife has MacHeath dear, and he keeps it out of sight.

The river is almost empty, the birds are calling to each other to come home, the light is failing, but still their eyes lock with each other from where she rests upon her elbows on the slippery seat cushion and where he stands, dipping backwards and up with the punt pole, and then forwards again to sink it into the muddy riverbed. She feels her fingers growing numb from the pressure on her elbows, a numbness that spreads through her like a soothing draught of poison, offered by a lover when he has no more to give. Meanwhile he turns the boat gently so that it noses against the riverbank, and then comes to a halt in the curve of an adventurous tree branch. He lies down beside her and begins to kiss her with a strange desperation, quite beyond the usual limits of his restlessness, she is too numb to respond.

Your hesitation is pure and beautiful, he says, it fills me with more sweetness than I can hold.

Suddenly, she puts her arms around his neck and pulls him very close to her, long ago, she says, long ago you showed me the way to find peace in my life, and in these six years since we parted I have painfully trudged upon that route, eschewing everything except what was intensely of value, forgoing human company unless it was touched by the nectar of the gods, and so bit by bit, I have built up a life which I can call my own, that I may inhabit without the need to be with you, or indeed anyone, a life where I might give shelter to all who care to grace it, but never demand their presence, their affection, their endorsement of my actions.

And now you have come to destroy all that I have attempted to create, to crush in your palms the fruit of the pain that I have nursed for so long, but if it must be so, so be it, for there is no one like you, and without you I can only call back the shadows of what I would have as my fate, only that these shadows are beautiful and mellow, and perhaps in some respects easier to live with than you, yourself, or so I have convinced myself, after so many years of waiting for you, and knowing that you would never come.

I remember, she says, when we first became truly aware of the awful depth of our love. We were having dinner some-where, and then you, as we were waiting for our coffee, you began to caress my palm, and this wrought within me an anxiety so sublime that when the power suddenly failed, and the darkness came rushing in between us, it was like a benediction. The waitress brought us candles, and by their dim light, you kissed my fingers, you kissed them with more yearning than could be contained in the small moments of our knowing each other, I knew then that you were a part of my destiny that nothing could deny.

And yet, all these years, I have been trying to find a way to cherish you without letting you consume me, and finally I have found someone with whom I might build a different kind of life, one of more mutual respect perhaps, for his motives are impeccable, unlike yours which are clothed in the sweet mercury of reflected sin.

My beloved, he says, kissing her upon her closed eyes, can you not keep me as a secret dream within you, a flow of lava beneath the quiet crater, never threatening, only there, free to bubble sometimes through some unwary crack and char you a little, but nothing more. Can you not go back to your saint, your holy mendicant, your strolling player, with me in your heart? Can you not return unsanctified to that temple, am I not worth that? For years, after all, I too have lived with the guilt of loving you, of thinking of you when I should have been thinking of my wife and my son, of wanting to relate some particularly interesting event in my life first to you and then to them, or to read a passage that affected me deeply to you before anyone else, it has not been easy for me, my love, it has not been easy.

But you have drowned your sorrows in the arms of other women, she says.

Does that really bother you? he asks.

Not in the slightest, she replies.

Because you know, he says, oh you know so well that you affect me like no other, it has driven me wild to think of how well you know this, for some part of me would like to keep you guessing, make you tear a field of daisies with the burning enigma – he loves me, he loves me not – but you have always known exactly what you mean to me.

It is that, and only that, which has kept me alive, she tells him.

I know, my love, I know, he says, tasting the salt of her tears.

She feels water seeping into her clothes, his cheek is upon hers, he is sighing deeply in her ear, no words will ever be said between them anymore, he traces the curve of her neck with his cold fingers, kisses the angle of her jaw, and then he turns abruptly so that the boat tips to one side, and they are spilled out onto the bank. He pushes the boat away with his foot, and it ambles slowly out into the middle of the river, and is carried away by the mild current, she watches its shadowy shape drift away, and then turns to look into his eyes, which are smiling, smiling, smiling.

When the shark bites with his teeth dear, scarlet billows start to spread, fancy gloves though wears MacHeath dear, so there's not a trace of red.

Debendranath Roy can still dimly see the river, he smells it in gangreneously green detail, as he waits by the boathouse with the others for more news, for the thin trickle of apprehension that he had felt when his niece had not come, as she had promised, in the evening to read to him, that slight thread of unease has thickened now into the ironic certainty that a punt that had returned unmanned was the very one she had hired earlier with a man that the police are now sure is Daniel Faraday, whom he has not seen since the day he dropped him off in his green racing car just up there, by the bridge. His parents have arrived, dumbfounded at this suspicion, for they did not even expect him to be in the country, he had sent no word that he was coming, but a phone call to Australia confirms that he had left suddenly on the day before yesterday – by their clock – he had taken a flight to London, but they were all unclear about the nature of his mission.

Has something happened to him? Alison had asked.

I do not know, Rosemary Faraday had replied, her head reeling, her throat dry. And now they were assembled on the banks of the river, with the police searching the truant boat, they have already found his keys upon its floor, and now a policeman hands Debendranath Roy a scrapbook that he has found beneath a cushion. Is this familiar to you? he asks. But he cannot read the cuttings, and his wife is too overwhelmed with horror and disbelief to help him. He hands them to Professor Faraday, who is standing beside him, staring grimly into the dark waters. What are they? he asks.

They are reports of your death, says the old man. My son put them together a long time ago.

I thought they might be, says Debendranath Roy.

The policeman walks towards them again, here is another thing we found, he says, handing them a hinged box. Professor Faraday puts on his glasses to examine it, it is a locket of some sort, he says, I do not recognize it. He gives it back to the policeman, who places it in the hands of Debendranath Roy, if I shine a strong light on it, will you be able to make out any of the detail, sir?

I do still have a little of my sight left, admits Debendranath Roy.

I'll get our most powerful torch, says the policeman.

He rubs his fingers over the smooth surface of the locket, it is like a well-sucked lozenge, he wonders what it might contain, and then the policeman returns, and his world is suddenly drenched in a fierce light, he sees the shape of a lyre and it is like the gauzy skeleton of a bird, bleached with age, refined by time, Debendranath Roy is overwhelmed with gratitude for its ethereal beauty, he knows it is the last thing he will ever see.